FIRST
CAST

Leonard M. Wright, Jr.

A FIRESIDE BOOK
Published by Simon & Schuster Inc.
New York London Toronto Sydney Tokyo

A Fireside Book
Published by Simon & Schuster Inc.
Simon & Schuster Building
Rockefeller Center
1230 Avenue of the Americas
New York, New York 10020
Published by arrangement with Nick Lyons Books.
FIRESIDE and colophon are registered trademarks of Simon & Schuster Inc.

Manufactured in the United States of America

10 9 8 7 6 5 4 3 2 1 Pbk.

Library of Congress Cataloging in Publication Data

Wright, Leonard M.
    First cast.

    "A Fireside book."
    1. Fly fishing.   I. Title.
SH451.W75   1987   799.1'2   87-31087

ISBN 0-671-64564-1 Pbk.

First Cast

The Beginner's Guide to Fly-Fishing

Contents

Foreword

It has always struck me as cruelly unfair that the reader always knows precisely who he is and how much knowledge he has while the long-suffering author never has a clue about who is going to pick up his book. I'm going to level the playing field, this time, by presuming to know who you are and what you're up to.

First, I'll assume that you're not an expert fly-fisher, but would fall into either the "beginner" or "intermediate" categories. This will allow me to omit a lot of hair-splitting, technical points that are nearly impossible to describe in print, anyway. I'll stick to the most important things you should know, do and *not* do to become a "very good" angler.

Second, I'm taking it for granted that you're right-handed simply because I happen to be. Therefore, in any instructions, I will refer to the right arm as the casting arm and to the left hand as the line hand. If you happen to be a south-paw, I apologize, but I'm sure that, by now, you're well adjusted to such high-handedness from the right.

Third, you may feel that I put too much emphasis on flowing, fresh water—brooks, streams and rivers. But I'm doing that on purpose because three-quarters of all fly-fishing is practiced on running water. Lake, pond and salt-water situations won't be ignored. However, I'll have to tailor the coverage to the type of fishing you're most likely to be doing.

Finally, this is not meant to be either arm-chair reading or an encyclopedia. There are already thousands of books giving vivid experiences and exhaustive details on every aspect of the sport. Some of the most useful of these are listed in Appendix 5. Rather, this is intended as a "first word." Tuck it in your pocket or vest and take it along when you go fishing. It's a small book, no bigger or heavier than the average fly box. I hope what's inside will catch you more fish than the contents of any fly box you ever carry.

1

Why Fly?

"How do I love thee? Let me count the ways."

—Elizabeth Barrett Browning

In the beginning was the fly rod—or at least its primitive ancestor. We have graphic proof that "fishing poles" are 5,000 years old or nearly as ancient as the fish hook itself. Early rods swung the hook out to where the fish were and hauled the captives back, and that is essentially all today's high-tech boron rods are accomplishing.

Other forms of casting are surprisingly modern and totally different. All cast a relatively heavy weight and here, the lighter the line, the longer the cast. The bait-casting, or revolving-spool reel is some 200 years old and the fixed-spool, spinning reel is only about 100. For centuries, fishing with a rod meant fishing with a fly rod of some sort.

Artificial flies aren't quite so ancient. We have written proof that they were in use nearly 2,000 years ago and they may be much older than that. Very early in the fishing game, anglers noticed that stream and river fish were extremely fond of the aquatic insects that lived in, and hatched out on, the water. They

3

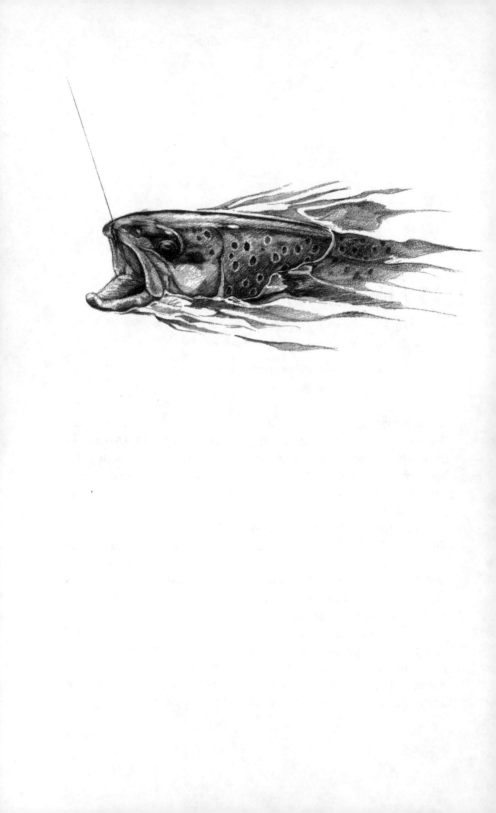

also discovered that these small, fragile mayflies, caddisflies and stoneflies turned into a gooey mess when they tried to impale them on a hook.

Some long forgotten genius concocted a fake fly by winding more durable feathers onto his hook and then played this in or on the water to act like the real thing. It worked—or worked often enough—and fly-fishing was born.

It was soon discovered that a long, limber rod helped to switch this fly farther out over the water. And experiments showed that a relatively fat, heavy line (except for a short, thin portion next to the fly) was needed to relay the energy of the rod and that the nearly weightless artificial fly would then go along for the ride.

Fly-fishing imposes several restrictions on the angler and yet, paradoxically, it is these limitations that make it so much more fun. The fly rod is a short-range weapon. Its maximum range is only a fraction of the surf casting rod's. It is also basically a shallow-water method. Admittedly, we now have fast-sinking and lead-core fly lines that permit some dredging, yet over 95

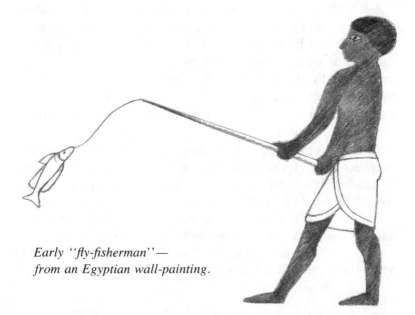

Early "fly-fisherman"—
from an Egyptian wall-painting.

A 16th-century English fly.

percent of all fly-fishing is done with floating lines that limit lure travel to the top layers of water.

A lure that is both near the angler and near the surface dictates a highly visual game. Frequently, you're casting to a fish, or its swirl, that you have observed. Often you can see the fish take your fly, as well. Seeing is half the fun in fishing. Few people enjoy night fishing. Fishing with a floating fly is widely considered the cream of the game. Not because it's in any way more sporting. It's just more visual. One take on the surface is worth two you merely feel.

Since you're casting at close range to seen or suspected fish the sheer luck of chuck-and-chance-it is also greatly reduced. Stealth, dexterity and, some might add, intellect are rewarded. Fly-rodding is thinking man's fishing.

Short and shallow doesn't mean you'll be short-changed in results, though. In many situations, fly-fishing is the deadliest method. A river I fish frequently flows into a large reservoir and where the current-flow starts to slow down marks a well known and heavily fished hot-spot for large, lake dwelling trout. Nearly every time I fish there, I enjoy the company of several spin-fishermen who are whizzing out the most popular lures. Yet I always (except when everyone goes blank because the fish haven't moved up in there) out-catch the bunch of them. Not because I'm a magician. A frequent companion who's a novice fly-caster outfishes them, too. Apparently the translucence and subtle pulsations of a good streamer fly make it a far more deadly imitation of a bait minnow than any wood or metal creation.

While fishing in France, I was fortunate enough to get to know, and fish with, a pair of local, professional trout fishermen. They made their livelihood by catching and selling the wild brown trout they caught from hard-pounded, public rivers. These anglers were frighteningly effective. French law, at that time, allowed them to use any bait or method short of gill nets and dynamite yet they chose smallish, insect-imitating flies 95 percent of the time to earn their daily *baguette*.

Fishing with flies can become an education in itself. The deeper you get into it, the more you'll want to learn. Your first step is likely to be collecting and studying the aquatic insects fish feed on. The next thing you know, you're into fly-tying, then on to poultry raising which can lead you into genetics to improve the stiffness and color of hackle feathers. Curiosity about stream fertility and habitat improvement pull you quickly into biology, water chemistry, geology, hydrology and forestry. The domino effects in fly-fishing can lead you down all sorts of primrose paths—and surprisingly enriching ones.

Not long ago, fly-fishing was considered elitist. Live-bait fishermen thought fly-fishers were snobs and, unfortunately, they were right in many cases. In late 19th-century England, fly-fishing, especially dry-fly fishing, turned into an ethical, even moral, issue. This pecksniffian purism quickly flowed across the Atlantic, polluting our shores—or at least the Eastern one—for decades.

Two factors started to change all this shortly after World War II. Newly developed synthetics, fiberglass for rods, plastic coatings for lines, and monofilament for leaders replaced the organic materials: bamboo, silk and gut. The new outfits were cheaper, tougher and virtually maintenance-free. This helped enormously to bring fly-fishing off its artificial pedestal and down to earth.

Then, too, there were now more people fishing for far fewer fish. Many decided to fish for fun rather than for food. This new philosophy brought many new recruits to fly-casting because it is the only fishing method that is a joy whether you catch fish or (God forbid!) not. Try dunking a worm from an anchored rowboat all day long and you'll see what I mean.

I could go on and on, but any list of fly-fishing's rewards and virtues pales before the late Arnold Gingrich's crisp pronouncement: "Fly-Fishing is the most fun you can have standing up."

2

Setting out and Setting up

"Ther ben twelve manere of ympedymentes
whyche cause a man to take noo fysshe . . .
the fyrst is yf your harnays be not mete
nor fetly made."

—Dame Juliana Berners

Most financial columnists I read complain that we Americans are compulsive consumers. We save less and run up more personal debt than the citizens of any other industrialized nation in the world, they say.

I'm now going to do my part in trying to reverse that trend. If you're about to take up fly-fishing, do not—repeat, do not—rush to your nearest tackle store and pig out. Resist the temptation until you've acquired more knowledge and some sort of casting style of your own.

Instead, try to borrow a decent outfit from a friend who's an experienced fly-caster. Don't be afraid to ask. After all, you're not begging for the loan of his wife or toothbrush. Just a rea-

9

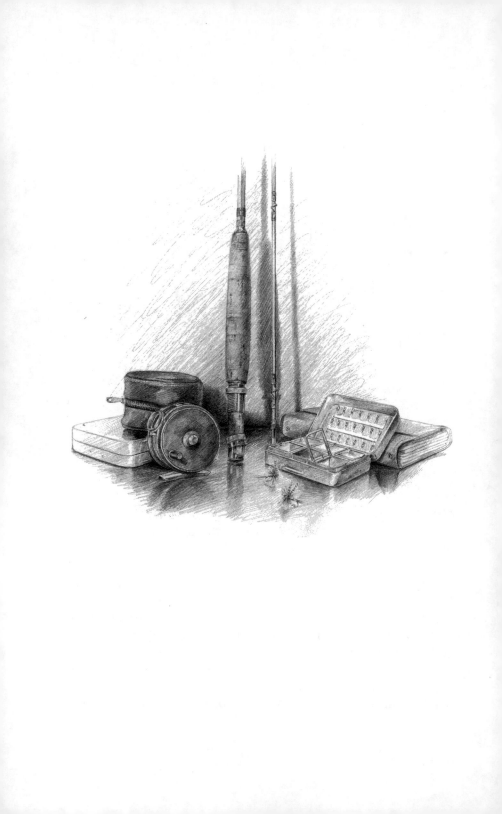

sonable fly-fishing outfit. The chances are he already possesses more of these than he'll admit to around the house, including some he hasn't used in years.

If he seems reluctant, go straight to gambit II. Suggest that he take you fishing so that he can personally supervise and safeguard his property. This is where you should end up anyway—free equipment plus free lessons. Only the most flint-hearted of fish-erpersons can resist such wheedling and cajoling. Fly-fishers are born proselytizers, all too willing to spread the faith.

RODS

The best or easiest rod to learn with is one that's relatively long and has a slow and forgiving action. I couldn't recommend one under eight feet and one of nine or more might be better if you have a choice. All things being equal, a longer rod bends more, making it easier for you to feel how it's working during the cast. A flabby rod is a disaster, but one with a ''slow'' action— meaning that it bends throughout most of its length instead of mainly in the tip-section—will help you feel the cast better, too.

LINES

The fly line must be matched carefully to the action of the rod. So important is this that rods are usually described by the line-weight they take as well as their length. The line-scale runs from the lightest, 1, up through the heaviest, 15. The code refers to the weight of the front thirty feet of that particular line. The lightest you're likely to encounter fall into the 3- to 4-weight class. Many prefer these for casting tiny flies on glassy limestone or spring creeks. Most rough-stream anglers choose slightly stouter outfits in the 5- to 6-weight range. Those who cast bulky streamer flies and bass bugs on still waters, seem to prefer 7- or 8-weights. Salt-water fly-casters usually choose rods that handle 8- to 10-weight lines and some, like those who cast for giant tarpon, swear by 12-weights.

All good fly lines are tapered. The most popular type, the

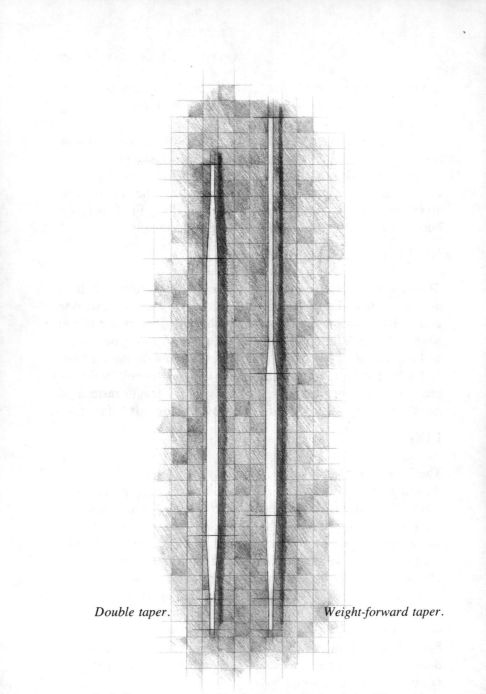

Double taper.   *Weight-forward taper.*

Both lines are greatly fattened to emphasize their differences.

double taper, starts out relatively fine, increases diameter gradually for six to ten feet then runs fat and level for most of its length before dropping down into a short taper again. With this type of line, if one end gets cracked or worn, you can reverse it on the reel and fish with an identical, unused section.

Weight-forward, bug or salt-water tapers are one-ended, though. They taper more quickly up to a fat, belly portion which, after about twenty-five feet, taper down into a thin running-line for the rest of their length which shoots more easily through the rod-guides. Despite some disadvantages, this type of taper helps you get casting line out quicker, gives you slightly more distance and makes casting bulky lures easier. The illustration compares these two basic line types.

REELS

Most fly reels are relatively simple affairs: they serve mainly to store the line you're not casting or holding in your left hand. A single-action model (one turn of the handle equals one turn of the spool) with a minimum drag will suffice for nearly all fresh-water fishing. For Atlantic salmon and large salt-water species, you may need a reel with a strong, adjustable drag, though in some cases, a multiplier (a reel in which one complete turn of the handle results in more than one turn of the spool) can come in handy.

LEADERS

Your leader should continue the taper in the front end of your fly line down to a thin section nearest the fly. You can buy ready-made leaders at most tackle stores. They come in many diameters and several lengths—nine feet being the most common. Some taper down to as fine as one-pound test while stouter ones, for salt-water use, may end up at twelve-pound test or even stronger. The size of the fly you're going to cast and the fish you expect to catch will dictate the size you put on that day. You'll also

13

Turle knot. The forward loop is pulled tight into a knot, then the rear loop is passed over the fly and tightened around the neck of the hook.

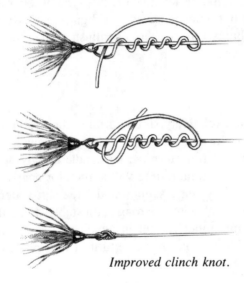

Improved clinch knot.

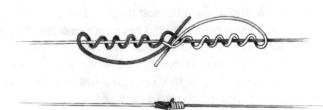

Blood (or barrel) knot.

need some spools of monofilament in several weight categories to vary the thickness of your tippet (the very end of the leader) or to renew it.

KNOTS

There are dozens of fishing knots, but for fly-fishing only three knots are essential. The improved Turle is best for up- or down-eyed hooks while the improved clinch is superior for staight-eyed models. For tying two pieces of monofilament together, use the blood knot. All three knots are fairly easy to tie with a bit of practice and the diagrams will show you how.

FLIES

We have now, finally, reached the business end of your tackle. The fly, after all, is the only part of your inventory that any fish should ever see. Flies come in all sizes, shapes and colors, but they can be grouped into five basic styles that are easy to recognize.

Dry flies are tied on light-wire hooks, have upright wings and a bushy collar of stiff hackle (rooster-neck feather) to help them float on the surface. Wet flies are usually tied on heavier hooks with wings and sparse, soft hackle sloping back toward the bend of the hook and are designed to sink quickly under the surface. So are nymphs, which are imitations of the larval stages of aquatic insects. These look much like wet flies without wings. Streamers (and bucktails) are large, long, and slim and represent various types of minnows. Lastly, bass bugs (and poppers) are big, bulky and are made out of deer hair, cork, balsa wood, hollow plastic or various combinations of these so that they will float on the surface. Some recommended patterns and sizes of all five types are listed in Appendix 2.

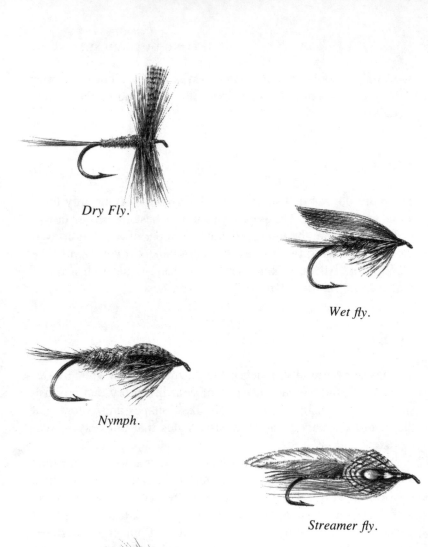

Dry Fly.

Wet fly.

Nymph.

Streamer fly.

Popping bass bug, with heavy piece of monofilament positioned as a weed-guard.

WADERS AND ACCESSORIES

Equipment for fly-fishing rarely ends with just the basic tackle, however. Since you're going to be on, or in, the water you'll need help in keeping dry.

In some cases, this calls for a boat. A canoe may be your best choice for small lakes or ponds. At the top end of the scale are blue-water sports-fishing boats that can cost up to half a million dollars fully equipped. It all depends on where you fish, how elegant you wish to be, and what you can afford.

More often, you'll need only hip-boots or chest-waders to separate you from the chilly water. Boots are fine for brooks and small streams. Larger streams, rivers, lake margins and surf usually call for waders. Whichever you end up with, get ones with felt on their bottoms where they come in contact with slippery rocks. They can spare you uncomfortable, sometimes dangerous, dunkings when you're negotiating slimy rocks. There are a few notoriously treacherous streams where metal cleats or chains are a virtual necessity. There are also some with sandy or gravelly bottoms where regular rubber bottoms are satisfactory, but, for all-around work, I'd put my money on felts.

You should have a good pair of glasses for eye protection, and Polaroid sunglasses, which cut the glare and let you see beneath the surface, are usually the best choice.

Fly-fishers seem to have a special weakness for accessories and gadgets. (Perhaps those hand-wringing economists are right, after all.) You'll find a list of necessities and sometimes-useful extras in Appendix 4. You decide how much you want to lug around.

RIGGING

Before you actually start fishing, you have to rig up your tackle and, even here, there are Do's and Don't's. There are several ways to knot or splice your leader to your fly line and this to the

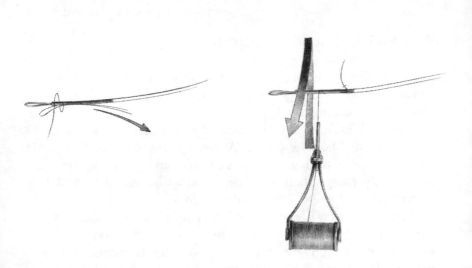

Wind several wraps of thread back over thread-end, then trim end. Wind several turns over thread-loop, insert thread-end through loop, then pull loop and thread through windings. Clip flush and varnish well.

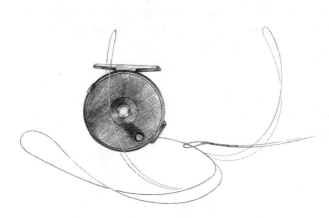

Insert backing-loop through smaller line-loop, pass backing-loop over reel, then pull tight.

fine backing-line that fills up your reel spool. All will slip through your rod guides easily, but there's a better way to make these connections.

Since nearly all leaders come with loops on their heavy ends, you can change them much more easily if there's a loop in the end of your fly line, too. Simply insert one loop through the other and pull the rest of the leader on through and you have a firm, neat attachment. The same system works for your line-to-backing linkage. The illustration shows you how to whip on these loops. I'd recommend a loop of 20-pound test monofilament for the leader end of your fly line. A small length of backing—that lighter, limper bait-casting line you use to fill up the reel spool underneath your fly line—makes a neater connection on the other end. Just double the backing line back on itself and fasten it into a loop by the same method. Make sure this is large enough— six to eight inches should do—to pass over the reel.

When stringing the line through the guides, double back the first few inches of fly line and poke this highly visible part through each guide in turn. You're much more likely to skip a guide if you try doing this with the nearly invisible monofilament leader. And, before you knot on your chosen fly, make a final inspection to make sure you haven't missed a guide or spiralled the line around the rod some place. It is surprisingly easy to foul up this simple process if you're trying to rig up when fish are rising all around you!

Now hook your fly in the first, or stripping, guide of your rod, run the leader around the rim of the reel and then reel in the slack until the line is tight. Don't put the fly in that small keeper ring many rod-makers place just in front of the grip. It's far more likely to hook one of your fingers there and it will also mash the hackles of a good dry fly.

Now that we're finally rigged up and headed for the river, here's a last tip. Carry your rod pointed forward: it's by far the easiest way during daylight hours. Tip pointed rearward may be safer for the rod when you're feeling your way back to your car after dark, but be forewarned, you'll hang up on far more twigs and branches that way. When you must carry the rod butt-first, make sure the line is still rigged through the guides and the hook is firmly attached. Otherwise, when your rod gets hung up in the bushes the tip section may get pulled loose and then it's lost and gone forever.

Preparing your rigged-up rod for along-stream travel.

3
Casting

*"The faults one naturally looks for in
a learner are taking the rod too far back
and not waiting until the instant when the line
is extended."*

—Eric Taverner

Casting with a fly rod, when done properly and automatically,
is one of the great joys of fly-fishing. Its motion is fluid, graceful,
gratifying and, like virtue, is a reward to itself. However, it takes
a lot of concentration and practice to become an expert caster
and it's not really easy to become even a good one.

For the complete novice, learning to cast well takes determi-
nation. Despite the fact that there are entire books devoted to this
art and that most start out with the assumption that the reader
has never cast a line before, I frankly don't believe that fly-
casting can be taught from scratch by printed words and pictures.
Get an experienced friend or a fishing school to help you through
the early stages. This will spare you hours of agony and frustra-
tion.

If this is, indeed, to be your very first try, string up the fly

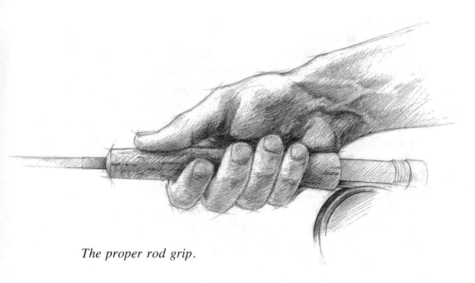

The proper rod grip.

rod, attach a leader of about nine feet and tie on a fly (preferably one with the point and bend snapped off) and pull twenty feet or so of line out beyond the rod tip. Now have your instructor/friend make several casts and explain carefully what he's doing. This will give you some inkling of what you're going to try to duplicate.

After a few of the basics have sunk in, take the rod in your own hand, grip it properly, thumb up, as pictured. Grasp it firmly, as you would a hammer. There's no need to clutch it like grim death: it's not likely to get away.

Now take a comfortable stance with your feet about a foot and a half apart and face 45 degrees to the right of the direction you intend to cast. You're now in position to execute the simple, overhead cast, which is the one you'll use most of the time.

THE OVERHEAD CAST

Don't try to cast solo, yet, though. Instead, have your experienced friend stand directly behind you and wrap his hand around yours. Relax your hand and arm while he does the casting for a while. You'll quickly get the feel of how much force he's using, how far he's moving the rod tip, how long he waits for the line to extend to the rear before starting the forward cast.

Gradually start participating in the casts by taking over part of the efforts of the coaching hand. Keep increasing your percentage of the power while your friend decreases his. At some point soon, a cast will probably fail—either slapping the ground or water behind you or falling in a heap in front of you. At that point, you should relinquish control to the instructing hand and try the sequence all over again. Twenty minutes to half an hour of this, with a running commentary from your coach, is about all you can absorb in one session. Only when you've made several good casts in a row while the instructing hand is passive should you start trying to cast on your own.

If you practice at regular intervals—just casting, no fishing— you'll improve rapidly and won't acquire some of the bad habits that are so hard to correct once they get ingrained. But that's probably asking too much. Once you get near the water, the temptation to fish is overpowering. If, however, you keep a clear mental picture of how and why a fly rod works, you may avoid the worst pitfalls.

THE HOW AND WHY OF CASTING

Fly-casting is actually a misnomer because you're not casting a fly at all. What you're really casting is the center of gravity of that portion of your line that's beyond your rod tip. If a fly line weren't relatively fat and heavy you couldn't cast it ten feet. Fly-casting works the way a bull whip does, with the energy carried along a traveling loop that delivers the fly as a by-product. What keeps the line in the air and keeps it unrolling is the speed or energy you give it. A rod helps you increase this line speed in two ways.

A fly rod is, in one sense, just a lever that lengthens your arm. Since the average forearm measures only about one and a half feet, if you held the line in your bare hand—without any rod at all—your hand would travel only about one and a half feet during the classic casting motion. Now add to this eight and a half feet of rod and the line can now be activated through ten feet of travel. If the hand-cast and the rod-cast are accomplished in the same amount of time, the rod-cast will create over six times as much line speed. (I once knew an expert who could cast thirty yards with his bare hand, but don't even *think* of trying it.)

The rod is also a simple leaf-spring that can store energy and release it with a quick snap. This imparts extra speed to the line in much the way a bent-back, plastic ruler can zip a spitball across the classroom.

If you keep these two essential functions of a fly rod in mind while you're casting, it may help you avoid the most common and crippling mistakes. Since your aim is to propel the line out in front of you (and, alternately, straight behind you), the rod, as both lever and spring, will be most efficient when it is positioned at a right angle to the line's direction of travel. In other words, your rod and your power stroke are most effective when the rod is vertical or nearly so. The most common cause of a bungled or sloppy cast is the powering of your cast when the rod has traveled back too near the horizontal position.

There's another excellent reason why power should be applied quickly and crisply when the rod is in the near-vertical position and not through a long, lazy arc. You want the unrolling loop in your fly line to be small. The tight loop formed by a high rod tip is far more efficient. It will cut through the wind resistance more easily, giving you either a longer cast or one the same length but with less effort.

Tight loop.

Open loop.

TIMING THE CAST

The second deadly sin in casting is starting to power your cast too quickly, before the line has straightened out behind or in front of you. For example, if the line-loop has only half-way unrolled behind you, only half of the weight of your line can act to bend your rod backward, building up energy for the forward cast. You'll be using only half the rod's potential as a spring and you will get some other nasty side effects, as well.

How long then, in terms of seconds or fractions thereof, should you pause for line-straightening? I'm afraid that's one of those questions in a class with ''How long should a man's legs be?'' You'll have to acquire that split-second, intuitive sense of timing through experience and practice.

Obviously, the longer the line you're casting, the longer you'll have to wait for it to straighten out. Unfortunately, you can't wait until you feel the rod being bent backward because, by then, it's too late to start the forward cast. Human reflexes just aren't quick enough for that. You'll have to start your forward power-stroke a mini-second before you feel that tug.

The best way to time your cast is by watching. Since your stance is opened up forty-five degrees to the right of your line of casting, it's easy to turn your body and swivel your head to observe your fly line as it travels behind you. I find that, with my casting style and reflex time, I have to start my forward stroke just before the highly visible fly line (you can't see your leader, usually) straightens out completely. You may find your best timing point occurs either slightly earlier or later. One thing is certain, though. When your timing has been perfect, you can feel the sweetness of it right down to your heels—just as you can when you hit a tennis ball in the dead center of the racquet.

Of course, even tournament casters don't time every cast absolutely perfectly. If you're only a tiny fraction early or late and you've done everything else properly, you'll still get a good, fishable cast. There's that much forgiveness in the system.

27

The back cast.

3.   2.   *1.*

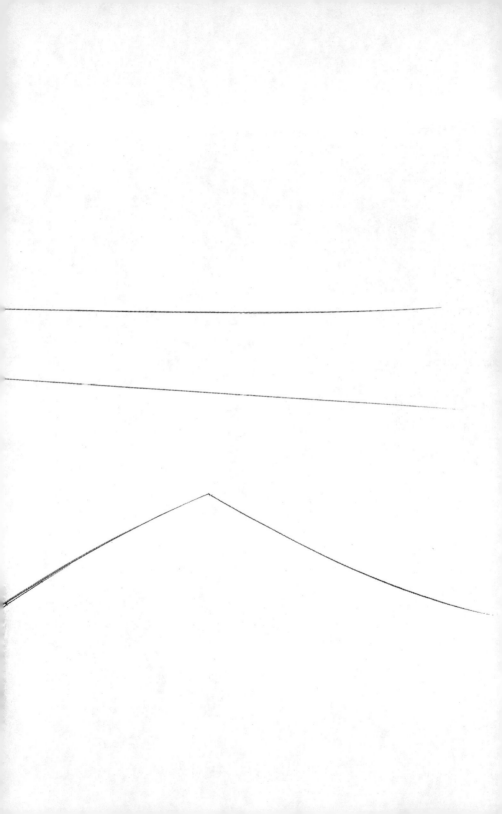

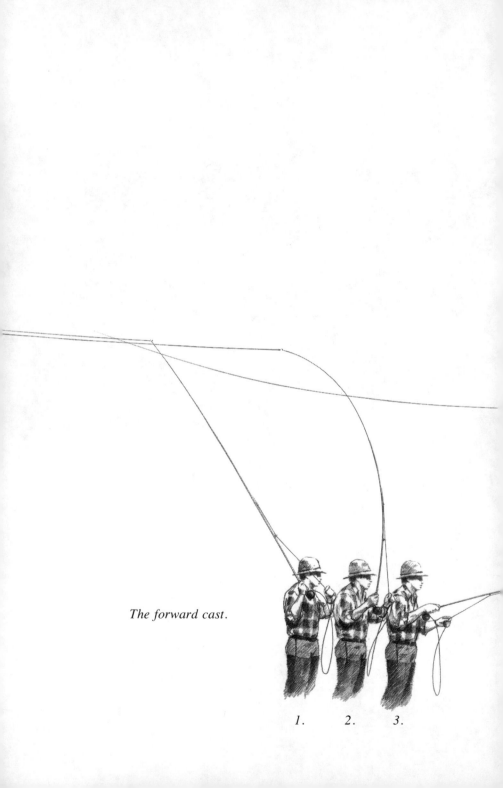

The forward cast.

1.   2.   3.

To increase the amount of line you're casting, pull more off the reel, hold this excess in your left hand and then feed it out through the rod-guides at the proper moment. In this way, several feet of line can be added on each stroke, forward or backward, while you keep the line aerialized, never touching the water. This is called "false casting" and is, by the way, an excellent practice exercise.

The only trick here is to know exactly when to let the extra line go. If you release a loop too soon, it can rob the traveling line of velocity, making the cast collapse. A good rule of thumb is to let line go only after the line-loop is at least half-way unrolled. This will insure that there's enough weight of line traveling beyond the rod tip to pull the new line handily through the guides.

This feeding-in of extra line can be done in quite large increments as long as extra power is added, too. If the line is coiled neatly and sufficient power applied, it's easy to "shoot" an extra fifteen, twenty or even more feet of line on the final, forward cast.

CASTING POWER

There are two distinct schools of thought on how you should power your cast. The old, or classic, school maintained that you should use the wrist almost exclusively. Pupils were made to practice while standing on cobblestones with a small, glass flask of whiskey pressed between elbow and side. They kept their arm-motion to a minimum or they went thirsty.

Some modern theorists claim you shouldn't use your wrist at all. They insist that your forearm, upper arm and shoulder should do all the work.

I'm not going to take sides because, as in most such cases, there's some merit to both theories. Tournament casters, striving for maximum distance, use not only their whole arms, but their backs and legs as well and some throw a fly an incredible distance that way. On the other hand, there's seldom any need to strain all those muscles because probably ninety percent of all trout are caught on casts of thirty-five feet or less. If arm and rod extend ten feet in front of you and the leader is nine feet long, only sixteen feet of fly line needs to be aerialized to reach out thirty-five feet. You can do that easily with a flick of the wrist. I find wrist-casting gives me a more delicate touch in presenting a fly at short range. It also tends to make rod motions shorter and crisper, keeping the rod near vertical during the entire cast. When I go for more distance, my arm and then my shoulder come into play readily enough.

THE ROLL CAST

The only other cast you'll need to master is the roll cast and this is far easier than the overhead one. You won't have to use this cast while fishing lakes, ponds or the ocean from a boat, but it's a godsend when trees, bushes or steep banks leave you no room for a back-cast.

In making the roll cast, you rip the line off the water rather violently and send it out again in a rolling loop. Point your rod straight down the line then raise it smoothly at medium speed until it has reached the one o'clock position or slightly beyond the vertical. Wait a split second until the line bellying in toward you slows and starts to sag then, instantly, make a strong forward power stroke. Your hand will try to slam the rod all the way down to the water surface to create more rod-tip travel, but you must resist this impulse. You have to stop the rod tip in a fairly high position to create a small, tight loop on the forward cast. In a few tries, you'll find out how long a line you can snatch off the water and aerialize with the outfit you're using.

Handy though it may be, the roll cast has some shortcomings. If you're casting with a sinking line, you'll find the roll cast somewhere between difficult and impossible to execute except for very short distances. You can snap a rod by trying to jerk too much sunken line out of the water.

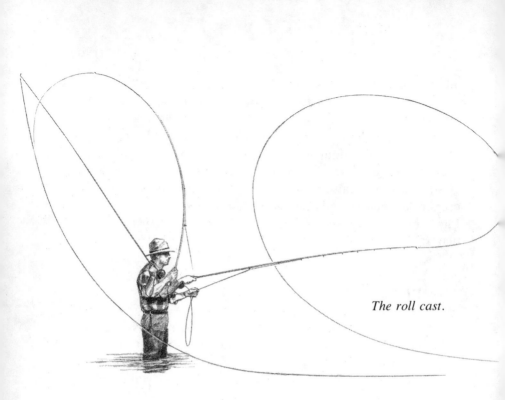

The roll cast.

A forward-taper floater is little better. It will come off the water surface easily enough, but you can make an effective forward cast only with the short, fat belly of the line. The thin running-line back of that won't transmit enough energy to power out the forward cast. That's one reason why the double-tapered floater is the best choice for most stream fishing.

The roll cast won't present your fly on the water as delicately or as accurately as the conventional one will. This is no great hardship when you're slamming out a streamer fly, but it can be frustrating when you're trying to present a dry fly properly. You can't get as much distance out of a roll cast as you can with the overhead cast, either. But when you have a wall of willows at your back and large fish rolling forty to fifty feet in front of you, the roll cast will give you at least a fighting chance.

TROUBLE-SHOOTING

In one way, casting is like golf: no matter how expert you become, errors will creep into your stroke. Even the most famous golfers have to engage another professional from time to time to tell them why they're driving so many balls into the rough. When you find you're botching too many of your casts, have a companion (preferably one who's more expert than you) watch you cast and pick out the flaws. If you're not yet very experienced, it's a good idea to get a regular check-up, anyway. Sometimes you can even do the trouble-shooting on your own. Some symptoms help you diagnose the disease.

All too often, your backcast will run out of steam half-way through the unrolling process and drop dead on the cobbles or slap the water behind you. This kills any chance for a decent forward cast. You may never in your lifetime catch a fish that's behind you, yet your backcast deserves every bit as much attention and rod power as your forward one does. If you make a flabby power-stroke through a wide arc and allow the rod to drift too far back from the vertical, you're asking for a wimpy backcast.

There is one other possible cause of a failed backcast, though. If there's too much slack in the line on the water in front of you, you'll have difficulty in loading up the rod to snap your line up and to the rear. This is seldom a problem when you've cast in a downstream direction because the current keeps tightening the line. But, when you're fishing a dry fly or nymph upstream, the current is constantly building in slack. The best way to foil this cast-spoiler, I've found, is to use a false roll cast on the pickup.

This sounds fancy, but it isn't. As the line travels down-current toward you, raise your rod straight and high to form a line belly, then execute the previously described roll cast. The only new wrinkle is that this time, as the line straightens out, but *while it is still in the air*, start your standard, overhead backcast.

If you hear a loud crack during your backcast, stop fishing and reel in. You have just snapped off your favorite fly. How could you possibly have done such a thing? By not waiting nearly long enough for the line to straighten out behind you before starting the forward cast. Remember, this is fly-casting, not crack-the-whip.

When your leader won't straighten out and deliver the fly properly, your hands won't smell very fishy at the end of the day. Occasionally, too light a fly line or an improperly tapered leader can be at fault. But, even with balanced tackle, it's all too easy to deposit your fly on the water amid slack coils of leader. Check for either of these two mistakes—or both: (1) a dying backcast or (2) applying your forward power-stroke too late and too low, creating an enormous line loop that runs out of energy before it can straighten the leader.

Sometimes your line will roll out over the water like a giant hoop, the belly of it landing on the surface several seconds before your fly does. This isn't a serious problem when you're fishing lakes and ponds where there are no currents, but it can be self-defeating on streams and rivers. If you're casting at right angles to the flow, that portion of your line nearest the rod tip will start moving downstream well before your fly hits the water. This will mean that, instead of lying on the water in a straight line, your fly line will have a huge, downstream curve in it which will whip the fly through the water at trout-frightening speed. And, even in upstream casting, that part of the line nearest you will hit the water prematurely, start hurrying downstream and will pull your late-arriving fly downcurrent at an unnaturally rapid pace.

This "hoop" syndrome can indicate that your cast has been only half wrong, which means that you're already showing improvement. Your back-cast may well have been high, tight-looped and properly timed. You went wrong in continuing your forward power-stroke too long and right down to the water surface. This can create a line loop ten feet in diameter and that portion of your fly line near the rod tip will hit the surface almost instantly.

While you're learning, it's a wise idea to examine your fly and leader every few minutes. If you've broken the point off your hook on the back-cast, the sooner you find out, the better. Even more frequently, you'll discover that some sorcerer has tied small knots in your leader. These so-called "wind knots"—usually simple, overhand knots—should be dealt with immediately. They reduce your leader's strength by about fifty percent. Pick them out with a needle or hook-point if you can. If you can't, tie on a new strand of tippet material. Neglect those knots and the biggest fish you'll see all year is sure to choose that moment to take your fly—and snap your half-strength leader.

These knots are thrown in because there was a "closed" or "tailing" loop in your fly line. The illustration shows you how this looks. And what causes this malformed loop? Again, starting the power-stroke of the forward cast too early—before the line has straightened out behind you. When you can fish an entire day without picking up a single leader knot, you're getting very proficient, indeed.

#@*! WIND!

Wind is the fly-caster's mortal enemy. It has caused more blasphemy than lost flies, broken rods and pratfalls into ice water combined. And yet, it is so frequent and ubiquitous, it has to be dealt with somehow.

A wind coming straight at you sounds like the worst-case scenario, but it's not. It will keep your back-cast up and straighten it sooner, reducing errors in that troublesome area. Then, if the wind is not too strong, you can make a good forward cast merely by adding power to your stroke.

There's another tactic that can help you cheat a head wind. Try the side-arm cast. I won't describe this in detail because it is made exactly the way the overhead one is and with all the same Do's and Don'ts. The only difference is that it's executed in a horizontal plane instead of a vertical one. The advantage here is that, due to friction with the earth's surface, wind velocity two feet off the water is usually only half what it will be ten feet up.

When the wind is coming from your left, you shouldn't have too much trouble, either. It will blow your line to the right, away from your head and body. You can still create a tight loop in your line on the forward cast if you angle the rod diagonally to the right on the forward stroke.

Wind blowing from your right is far more annoying. As the line passes overhead on the back-cast, it will tend to hang up on the rod or on your head and shoulders. If this happens, bring the rod back over your left shoulder when you pick the line off the water for the back-cast, pause, then make your forward cast in the normal manner, in line with your right shoulder. Line, leader and fly will then pass you safely on the leeward side. This may create a wider, less efficient line loop, but it beats getting hooked in the ear. (By the way, always wear a hat and some sort of glasses when fly-casting. A hook in the scalp can be painful, one in the eye a tragedy.)

The nastiest wind of all is the one that blows from behind you. It beats down your back-cast, makes it slow to straighten out and multiplies the chances of your making the greatest mistakes. There are three counter-measures against this ill wind, but they are only partial ones. First, try a side-arm back-cast to keep the line below the worst of the wind. Second, back-cast a much shorter length of line. You can make up some of the lost distance by shooting extra line downwind. And third, add extra power— but *not* extra rod-tip travel—to your backward stroke. If you use all three tactics, you still won't achieve the range or delicacy you'd expect in a dead calm, but you'll be able to hang in there.

All very well, but what do you do when the wind at your back is gusting up to near gale force? I'm afraid your only resort then is the roll cast. (And what heroic roll casts you can make downwind!) But perhaps it's wiser to reel in and quit. Fish seldom feed, or take flies, well when the wind is blowing that hard and we'll see why in the very next chapter.

Where to Fish—
and When

*"It's ill work fishing when the fish'll no' take;
and it's worse when they're no' there."*

—Quoted by
Lord Grey of Fallodon

Now that you've learned *how* to cast, the next step is to figure out *where*. Izaak Walton himself couldn't catch one undersized chub if he were casting where there weren't any fish. On the other hand, if he knew the hot spots, the village idiot could fill his creel. There's a strong hunting element in fly-fishing.

Sometimes fish give themselves away, as when they, or the swirls they make while feeding, can be seen in shallow water. All too often, though, your quarry is not that obliging and, when you peer out over the water surface, you feel like you're looking for a needle in a whole field of haystacks.

Fortunately, fish are self-serving creatures controlled by three basic drives: food, comfort and safety. Knowing this is a fine headstart, but it doesn't answer all the specifics. Which species

Brown trout sheltered under a log.

of fish are out there? What kind of food do they eat? Where does their food hang out? What water temperature does this gamefish prefer? And where does it feel safe—under a rock, in a weedbed or in deep water? You'll need answers to whittle down the odds against you. I warned you that fly-fishing was a thinking man's game.

You are probably already familiar with the types of gamefish that inhabit nearby waters. When visiting new territory, you can readily pick up this information from the local tackle store or bait shop. And the arrivals of seasonal, migratory, salt-water species are usually announced in the outdoor columns of the daily newspaper.

Information on food, temperature and habitat preferences are harder to come by. You'll find general rules of thumb for some of the most popular gamefish in Appendix 6, but they're only the bare essentials. You should study up on any species that's of special interest to you.

READING RUNNING WATER

Streams and rivers are the most important resource because they're shallow-water habitats and have the heaviest concentrations of the aquatic insects that make up the foundation of fly fishing. Many types of gamefish inhabit running waters, but by far the most important are the several species of trout: brook, brown, rainbow and cutthroat. All these have basically the same habits and requirements. Shad, salmon and sea-running trout migrate up our coastal rivers, but their distribution is so limited that we won't go into them here. Smallmouth bass are, however, a fairly common stream-dwelling fish, even though they take a back seat to the trouts.

In a stream environment, trout behavior is strongly territorial. This means that once a fish has found a suitable lie in the river, he'll stay there, repelling smaller challengers, for most of the season. This characteristic insures that trout will be fairly evenly

Rainbow trout.

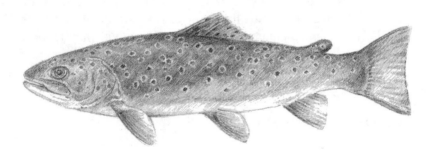

Brown trout.

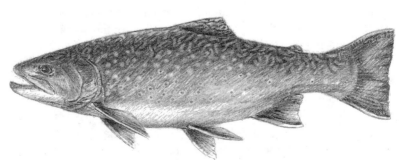

Brook trout.

distributed throughout the fishable length of a stream. You won't find a large school in one pool, then nothing for the next mile, for example.

When you take a good fish from a certain lie, mark the place carefully. Another fish is almost certain to move into that choice spot within a day or two and you'll know exactly where to cast.

Early in the season, when water temperatures are still in the 40s, and again in the fall when water cools down, trout will huddle in slow, deep pools. On opening day and for a few weeks thereafter, it pays to concentrate on the slowest, deepest water you can find. Trout rarely feed actively until the water hits forty-five degrees and they turn off again when it heats up to over seventy degrees. Smallmouth feeding range is about five degrees warmer. It's wise to carry a stream thermometer with you. It can save you a lot of wasted time and effort.

Once the readings get up into the mid-fifties, many trout will leave the pools for faster water—runs, riffles and pockets where they will remain until autumn's chill sends them back to the wintering holes. The warming waters of spring make for classic fly-fishing because, during this period before full summer sets in, the hatches of aquatic insects are the heaviest of the year.

In late spring and summer, trout feed in predictable places where they'll wait passively for the endless belt of the current-flow to bring them their food. That's why they'll position themselves in the tongue of a current where the most food is funnelled to them.

Trout, at least decent-sized ones, have one other criterion for selecting a lie. In all but the largest, deepest rivers, they need a sanctuary—a safe-house to hide in when threatened. In addition to anglers that stumble through their waters, trout are harrassed by ospreys, herons and king-fishers from above and by mink, mergansers and larger relatives from below. Their refuge may be a root-tangle, undercut bank or rock they can squeeze under. Where you find a concentration of such places, you should find excellent fishing. When a trout's in a mood to feed, it will drift

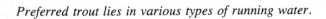

Preferred trout lies in various types of running water.

out of its hiding-hole and take up a station in the thread of a nearby current.

Some typical, preferred lies are pictured. Outsides of bends make ideal trout territory because most of the current, and therefore most of the drift-food, will be concentrated there. The digging force of floodwaters strikes hardest here, too, so this outside rim will provide deeper, safer water.

Trout also have a fondness for "pockets"—those mini-pools that are dug out behind large boulders during high water. Here they can find shelter under the overhanging sides of the rounded boulder and dart upwards to grab any morsel that drifts by.

One of the choicest places for both trout and fishermen is near the head of a pool where the inrushing water slows and deepens. Insects carried down from the food-rich riffle above are easy targets here and the deeper water gives fish a sense of security.

Deep runs can be productive, especially during hot weather. White-water chutes may be too fast for trout comfort, but deep glides with standing humps on their surfaces can hold fine trout—especially rainbows. Those big bumps in the current-flow indicate there's a sizeable rock under the surface which checks the water speed near the bottom where the trout will hold while the main current races by overhead.

Eddies or small whirlpools are formed where water enters a pool faster than it can empty out at the bottom, or downstream, end. In such cases, the current along one, or both, banks will flow, for a distance, in the "wrong" or upstream direction. Trout may, or may not, be lazy, but they certainly prefer to dine with a minimum expenditure of energy. A slow, counter-current acts like a lazy-Susan, serving the fish and often bringing the same morsel around several times before it can exit the pool. Given reasonable depth or cover, eddies may often contain more feeding fish than the main downstream current.

There's one last location I should point out because, at first glance, it seems an unlikely one and many anglers pass it by. I'm referring to shallow tails of pools. Fish do avoid such exposed lies during daylight hours, but, from dusk until pitch dark, the

45

Likely lies of lake and pond fish.

best fish in the pool may feed here. On summer evenings, flies that have mated and laid their eggs float down-pool, dead or dying on the water surface. Trout, once the light has faded enough to give them courage, often drift down to the slow shallows to gorge on these easy pickings.

Of course, these are only a few of the most typical places where you'll find good trout. There are too many minor variations and combinations to describe them all in detail. But, if you keep on the lookout for food-concentrating currents, reasonable depths and nearby cover, you should find enough trout to keep you busy.

READING LAKES AND PONDS

Still waters are harder to "read" than flowing ones. There are no obvious currents crinkling the surface to show you where the food is gathered. Lake fish don't get the "room service" river fish enjoy. They have to cruise around to find their meals and moving targets are notoriously elusive.

Still waters also, as they say, run deep—making it hard for the angler to see what's below. Only occasionally is it possible to make out the weed beds, boulders or bottom structure you're casting over.

The most common fly-rod gamefish in this environment are largemouth and smallmouth bass, pike, pickerel, sunfish, perch and, of course in cooler waters, trout. It's usually wisest to pursue one species at a time. With the possible exception of the small-bass-and-panfish combination, each type of fish will occupy slightly different territory and prefer a special type of food. Again, Appendix 6 will provide some starting pointers on this topic.

Admittedly, some fish will be out of the fly-rodder's reach some of the time. In mid-summer, trout may stay in the depths and even smallmouth bass can be too deep in some weather. You may be able to reach down a ways with a fast-sinking line, but dredging over ten feet deep with a fly outfit can be arduous work

47

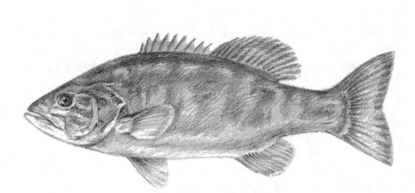

Smallmouth bass.

Largemouth bass.

for marginal results. I never promised you fly-fishing could catch all of the fish all of the time.

Clues to what lies under lake and pond surfaces are seldom provided by the water itself. More often, the tip-off comes from the terrain that surrounds it.

Where a steep hillside plunges into a lake, this contour should continue under water so expect considerable depth near shore. If there's a cliff on the shoreline, you should, again, find deep water below it plus a rocky or rubble bottom that smallmouths prefer. In fact, rocky or rock-strewn shorelines of whatever pitch tell you to expect underwater rocks or boulders.

Where the land slopes gradually into the water, look for shallows to extend well offshore. If there are reeds, arrowheads or lily-pads close to shore, you may have found prime pickerel territory. Farther out, in five to ten feet of water, there could also be underwater weedbeds that attract Northern pike, but you'll have to use your polaroid glasses to locate them.

Points of land jutting out into a lake should get special attention. Fish cruising along the shoreline at varying depths have to pass through a relatively small area off the tip of a peninsula. Such a funnel for moving fish increases the odds in your favor.

Coves, which offer shoreline protection from most wind and waves, are favored by frogs and the young of many types of fish. Largemouth bass, attracted by this food supply, are especially fond of such places. If there are also weedbeds and depths of five feet or more, expect pike to hang out here, too.

Underwater reefs and islands are prime spots and easy to find when they're marked by buoys to warn off motor boats. If they're deep enough not to need marking, you'll have to search them out when there's good light and an unruffled surface.

Wherever a brook, stream or river enters still water, not only is extra food brought in, but the current itself also seems to attract some fish. Soon after ice-out, large schools of gamefish-attracting smelt will hang out near the mouth, waiting to push up into the current for night-time spawning. And, in the fall, trout and land-locked salmon will concentrate here, prior to their own spawning run.

READING SALT WATER

Salt-water gamefish are usually the most difficult of all to locate simply because the territories you have to prospect are so vast. In northern waters, your quarry will usually be an essentially schooling species—striped bass, bluefish or mackerel. When you find a school feeding near the surface, fishing can be spectacular. On the other hand, be advised there will also be enormous fishless vacuums between such concentrations of fish.

Wheeling, diving sea birds are a sure sign that a school of baitfish has been driven to the surface by larger fish just below. This is the ideal fly-fishing situation. Approach cautiously and quietly if you're in a boat so you won't alarm the gamefish and drive them away or down into deep water.

In some locations, you can depend on currents to help you pinpoint likely places. Tides, lacking in fresh-water situations, are the ocean-angler's ally.

Where a tidal pond empties back into the ocean marks a choice location. Such ponds are nurseries for all types of marine life. On a falling tide—especially the last half when currents are strongest—shrimps, crabs, sand eels and minnows will pour out with the flow, creating a popular "free lunch" for waiting game-fish.

A similar situation is created by a tidal river or creek. Here you have the additional factor of fresh or brackish water influence which is especially attractive to striped bass in the north and to tarpon, snook and other species in the far south.

Wherever there are tides of at least several feet and there are flats or islands obstructing water-flows, you'll find strong currents at certain tidal stages that concentrate opportunistic gamefish. If a stream of shrimps, swimming crabs or bait minnows pours through a narrow cut on a making or falling tide, predators will have discovered the place long before you stumbled onto it. Any condition that creates a food funnel is money in the sea-angler's bank.

Striped bass.

Another way to increase your percentages is to use the fly rod as a back-up rather than a primary technique. Many anglers troll or surf cast to locate feeding schools, holding their fly rod in reserve until they hit pay dirt. A fly rod is easily stowed in boat or beach buggy. When fish start slashing on the surface nearby, a quick switch of weaponry can be made. Unfortunately, when you're blind-prospecting over large areas, a fly rod provides the least efficient method of water coverage.

FLATS

The long rod comes into its own, though, when fishing southern or tropical flats. These large areas of thin water covering sand or turtle grass are hunting grounds for bonefish, permit, small barracuda, redfish and sometimes, mutton snapper. Here you cast only to seen fish or their swirls and the fly rod, delivering the likeliest, quiet-entry imitations, can be the most telling instrument.

As a general rule, fish move up onto the flats on a rising tide and fan out, looking for crabs, shrimp and other types of *delicatessen*. There are variations, though. Each flat seems to be

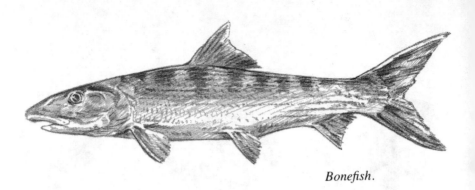

Bonefish.

governed by a slightly different set of rules. Until you learn the patterns and pecularities of your nearby flats, you're better off with a local guide to show you the ropes.

WHEN TO FISH

When you fish—on which day and at what hours—can be as crucial as where you cast. Disappointingly, fish don't feed well every day or all day. Unless you're rich, retired, enormously patient and have the arm of a blacksmith (and possibly all four) you'll want to focus your efforts on prime times.

One of the oldest and most widespread bits of misinformation holds that dark, drizzly days are best for fishing. Nothing could be farther from the truth. Bright, crisp, blue-sky days when the barometer is high or rising are head, shoulders and pectorals above windy, rainy, cloudy ones. You know you feel friskier on such days and so, for some reason, do the fish. If the weekend weather forecast calls for wind and rain on Saturday, but clearing on Sunday, do the long-promised household chores on Saturday and play hookey on Sunday.

Even the most beautiful, bluebird day, however, is like the proverbial curate's egg: only "parts of it are very good." In mid-summer, it may grow light at five o'clock and not get dark until after nine. Which of these sixteen long hours will be the most productive?

Much depends on the time of year, of course. Early or late in the season, when temperatures may be on the low side for the species you're after, it's wisest to fish during the heat of the day—say from noon till four o'clock. Sun is the main warmer of water, moving or still, fresh or salt. A sunny day, early or late in the season, means fish metabolism, and appetite, will peak when temperatures do.

Running water heats up, or cools off, more rapidly than larger, deeper ponds, lakes or bays. This is because streams, being shallow, moving ribbons of water, pick up heat from the sun-warmed stones on the bottom quite quickly during daylight and are cooled by the night air striking its high surface-to-volume ratio after nightfall. I have seen good-sized streams heat up, or cool off, by at least eighteen degrees in one day—a temperature change that could take weeks in the body of a lake or the bosom of the ocean.

This is why a thermometer is so valuable to stream-fishers. If we take the biologists' word that 63 degrees is the optimum temperature for trout feeding and that 68 is best for smallmouth bass, temperature readings can help you find the top feeding hours. Let's take a trout stream, for example. If the water temperature is only 57 degrees when you arrive at nine o'clock on a sunny day, you'll know that good fishing is just ahead of you, about an hour or two away, when the temperature has pushed upward near 63. Similarly, if, on that same day, you get a reading of 68 at five in the afternoon, you'll know that the next good fishing period will occur in the evening, when the sun goes off the water and it starts cooling down again toward that magic, 63-degree figure.

Lakes and ponds won't show such a wide swing in daily water temperatures even though their smaller changes may also influence fish-feeding times. Perhaps more important to the shallow-water fly-fisher are time of day and light intensity. Smallmouth bass, for example, may stay relatively deep during midday in summer to avoid the bright, overhead light. However, since most of the food is produced in the relatively shallow lake-margins, they'll cruise in within fly-rod reach during the evening and should still be there in the early morning hours. Trout in lakes show much the same pattern in late spring or fall, but may not make this journey at all during July and August if the shallows get well up into the 70s. Pike, pickerel and most panfish, which seem anchored to their favored habitat, may be more obliging and remain in reachable, shallow water all summer long.

Salt water has several sets of rules. Fish often stay out of the littoral zone, where they could be vulnerable to fly-rodding, during the sunny hours. This may be due to the increasing number of swimmers and boaters using the shoreline. Reports indicate that there were more gamefish foraging in the shallows during the day back in the 20s and 30s than there are in the 80s.

Because of this trend, which seems more pronounced in the north, your chances with the fly rod are best at dusk and again at dawn. Even if you're offshore in a boat, these are still your prime times. When the light is dim, fish find it easier to see their prey above them, against the lighter sky. At this hour, they'll often drive schools of baitfish up to the surface where they'll slash at them from below. Here, they're easy to spot and they're perfect targets for your fly rod. Of course, they're also likely to stay within your reach all night long, but I really can't recommend fly-fishing when it's pitch dark.

Some southern waters—especially the flats—can give you just the opposite situation. Blind casting here is out of the question. When you're poling or wading over these shallows you have to see your quarry, or at least its shadow or swirl. You need good light for this and the higher the sun, the better. From about nine o'clock in the morning until four in the afternoon are your best hours. Even so, if it clouds over or the wind kicks up, your chances are greatly reduced.

Fish that feed up on the flats give you one last opportunity in case you haven't had enough during the bright hours. Often they'll move into even shallower water, just a few inches deep, in the hour before darkness. Here you can see their tails as they nose down for food and sometimes the water is so shallow you can

54

see their backs as they cruise along. They're extremely spooky when they're in such shallow water. The spin fisherman, with his heavier, splashier lure or bait, doesn't stand a chance here. But the fly-rodder is at the top of his game.

5

The Approach

"Getting there is half the fun."

—Cunard Line

The fly-fisher should try to get as close to a fish as he can, without, of course, running the risk of alarming it. Close range should make your cast more accurate, your presentation better controlled and setting the hook far easier. You may be able to get within fifteen feet of a trout upstream of you in choppy water and you should do so if you can. On the other hand, you may not dare to get any closer than fifty feet to a bonefish in shallow water. Fish-stalking is an exciting part of fly-rodding and you'll soon learn what you can, and can't, get away with under various conditions.

In all cases, when you're approaching a seen or suspected fish, try to be stealthy. Gamefish sense they are more vulnerable when they're in the shallows or near the surface. It doesn't take much of a ripple, noise or motion from a nearby angler to send them bolting out of reach. Whether you're wading or fishing from a boat, there are several things you can do to make your presence less detectable.

Sneaking up to a small pool.

RUNNING WATER

When fishing streams and brooks—especially small, clear ones
—a clumsy entry into a pool can render any subsequent casting
a sheer waste of time. On these intimate waters, if you startle a
small fish out of the shallows, it can spread the alarm, Paul
Revere-style, to all the other residents when it charges up the
pool. Always look, plan and scheme before you step into a stream.

Fish in larger rivers are usually less spooky, but it still pays
to stalk them with respect. They can't hear your above-water
voice, no matter how loudly you shout, but they can hear a pin
drop under water. Don't scuff your feet and stay off teetering
rocks that could send a warning noise ahead of you.

Fish have a blind spot directly to their rear. Since stream-
dwelling fish always head into the current, this allows you to get
quite close to fish upstream of you. Crinkled water obscures a
fish's above-water vision and lets you get even closer. However,
when you're fishing a sunk fly across and downstream toward
fish facing in your direction, it's wise to cast a fairly long line.

A slow, quiet pool calls for extra caution. Glide into position
slowly and gracefully. If you send out rings of tell-tale ripples,
fish will be alerted. They may not dive under a rock or race
upstream, but they probably won't look at a fly, either, for fifteen
to twenty minutes after becoming suspicious.

It's always wise to stay as low as possible, even if you have
to crouch. Never allow yourself to be silhouetted against the
skyline. There's little advantage in wearing camouflage, but do
avoid light-colored clothing. A white hat is the worst thing you
can put on your head. Avoid any unnecessary motions—especially abrupt ones—and try to advance directly toward a fish.
This will make your approaching form appear nearly motionless.
And don't be too proud to kneel while casting.

You may think the act of wading is as simple as merely walking
through water, but it's not. Most underwater stones are slippery
and big, flat ones are notoriously so. Avoid them wherever possible. Try to plant your feet on the fine gravel that collects between

larger rocks. And resist the temptation to wade out deeper by using the tops of underwater boulders as stepping stones. That's risky business. If you must try it, be sure you have a change of clothing nearby.

Strong currents can make wading difficult, but there are ways to reduce their force. Stand sideways to the flow. Your legs and body offer less water-resistance in this position. (That's also a good point for ocean-waders to remember when they see an especially large wave bearing down on them.) Move one foot at a time and only when that one is securely planted should you move the other one. Move the upstream foot first then bring the other up next to, but never ahead of, it. A wading staff, or one improvised from a stout stick, can be a big help in high, fast water. The best wading advice of all, though, is "when in doubt—don't."

BOAT FISHING

Most lake and salt-water anglers usually operate out of some sort of boat and I'll have to assume you're proficient at handling your chosen craft. It's not within the scope of this book to teach you how to paddle your canoe or dock your forty-eight-foot Hatteras.

There are, however, several specialized Do's and Don't's that the boater-turned-fisher should keep in mind. First of all, study to be quiet. Ship your oars or put down your paddle noiselessly when you're approaching fish. Lower your anchor softly, too. Any splash or thump will put nearby fish on the *qui vive*. I once spooked a school of bonefish that were over a hundred feet away by clumsily dropping my Zippo onto the bottom of a Whaler.

If you're using a motor, turn it off well before you reach the intended fishing area, then coast or scull your way in. A few species of fish may seem undisturbed by engine or propellor noises, but most of them know better.

In choppy water, waves slapping against the side of your boat can alert nearby fish. You can sometimes cut down this annoyance by pointing your boat bow-first into the waves. And, of course, in a flat calm avoid sending out advance-warning ripples.

In the shallows or on the flats, the boat angler has an advantage over the wader. He has a higher viewing point and can pick out fish at a greater distance. On the other hand, fish can spot him from farther away, too. Even here, it sometimes pays to cast from a crouch or a kneeling position. And don't try to get as close to a fish as you might when you're wading.

6
Presentation

"Be still, moving your flies upon the water."

—Izaak Walton

Even though you have dropped your fly onto the water at precisely the right time and place, you still have to convince the fish that your offering is, indeed, lean red meat and not just a fraudulent bunch of fur and feathers. Exactly what you now do or, rather, make your fly do, will depend on what sort of food you're trying to imitate and what species of fish you're trying to fool.

DRY FLY ON RUNNING WATER

The dry, or floating, fly is one of the most effective lures for stream fishing because heavy concentrations of insects hatch out on, or fall onto, the water surface here and are eaten by trout. It is also the most visually exciting method of fly-fishing. A take on the surface means that you'll not only see a swirl or a ring on the water, but probably also the fish itself.

The best practice is to select an artificial fly that matches, as

63

Presenting a dry fly upstream.

Capture a live fly, then try to match it from your fly box.

closely as possible, the size, color and shape of the natural insects you see, or expect to see, on the water. All dry flies should be anointed with some type of floatant—paste, liquid or spray—so that they will float as high and as long as possible. And, before you start fishing in earnest, check that particular fly's stance on the water. Cast it a short way up-current and look it over carefully as it floats down past you. An occasional fly that looked great in your box will fail to sit well on the water. Some flop over, unappetizingly, on their sides. Worse still, a few may insist on floating on a vertical, rather than a horizontal, plane with tail and body submerged. Now—before you've wasted a half-hour casting it—is the time to discard that rogue fly and tie on another.

The conventional method of presenting a dry fly calls for a cast in an upstream or up-and-across-stream direction landing the fly about two feet directly up-current from where you saw either a fish or its rise-form. This should allow the imitation to float back downstream like a natural insect. If it skitters or drags across the current unlike the real flies on the water, trout will usually let it pass by, untouched. However, there are a few, but only a few, occasions where it pays to break this rule.

There are some choice places which simply can't be covered from a downstream position. Lies just upstream of major snags or large trees that have been toppled out into the stream-flow can only be reached from up-current. Stand nearly directly upstream from the fish and let the fly coast down to it on a slack line. Of course, you run the risk of alarming the trout when you pull the fly back at the last moment so that it won't get caught in the branches. However, this trick works often enough to be a valuable tactic and some of the best fish in any stream occupy these hard-to-reach places.

On other occasions, you may have floated your fly several times over a fish that continues to rise, but ignores your artificial. This usually calls for a change to a better imitation, yet even this doesn't always bring the desired result. As a last resort, give your fly a tiny twitch—only enough to make it twinkle on the surface—just before it passes over the fish. This often convinces a trout that, even though your fly looks a bit different from the ones it's dining on, it is, at least, alive and good to eat, too.

DRY FLY ON STILL WATER

There's little reward in fishing a dry fly on lakes and ponds unless you see fish actively surface-feeding. There's just too much blank territory to prospect with an almost stationary fly. But when fish are rising—and this is quite common on calm evenings—it's the most enjoyable way to catch trout, bass or panfish.

The traditional method is to cast your fly as close to a rise-form as possible and let it sit for ten or twenty seconds. If it goes untouched, make it jiggle on the water-surface then pause again after this small advertisement. You can usually repeat this procedure several times before the fly becomes drowned. At that point, pick it up and dry it out with a few false casts; then send it out to another likely spot for a repeat performance.

BASS BUGS AND POPPERS

Although these lures are fished on the surface, I can't really call them dry flies—even those that are tied up out of deer hair and then clipped to shape. In fact, only a few of the smaller "bass bugs" imitate any kind of bug. Most of them are supposed to look and act like frogs or injured minnows dying on the surface.

You do present bugs much as you would dry flies, though. You cast them out, let them sit for half a minute, jiggle them a bit and wait again. You follow the same procedure with a cup-faced popper only you give this a sharp tug each time to create extra surface disturbance and the loud "pop" that attracts fish from quite a distance. Frog imitations are fished differently and a bit faster. Catch a medium-sized frog and toss him out thirty feet from shore. He'll teach you far better than I can how to make your retrieve.

When fishing for bass and panfish, slow and seductive does it. Most anglers fish these floaters too rapidly. That agonizingly long pause between twitches or tugs really pays off.

On the other hand, when you expect pike or pickerel, speed things up. For some reason, a frog or minnow imitation that appears frightened and eager to leave the vicinity in a hurry seems to excite the killer instinct in these slim, toothy predators.

WET-FLY AND NYMPH ON STREAMS

The nymph is a relatively recent fly designed to imitate the underwater, or larval, forms of several aquatic insects, mainly mayflies, caddisflies and stoneflies. Wet flies, especially the soft-hackled, no-wing, models, are probably mistaken for nymphs, too, though some of the gaudier, winged patterns may suggest tiny fish or fry.

Both of these small, sunk flies are usually fished in essentially the same manner. The standard, and easiest, method is to cast them across and slightly downstream and let them swing with the current through a wide arc on a tight line until they hang in the current straight below you. If you take a step or two downstream after each cast and repeat this process, you can cover virtually all the likely water in a run or pool on a fair-sized stream in a surprisingly short time. This classic, ''chuck-and-chance-it'' approach may call for minimum finesse, but it is enormously productive—perhaps because the fly passes over so many fish.

There are, of course, infinite variations on this basic theme. The best wet-fly fisherman I know casts his fly slightly upstream, letting it sink and drift for fifteen or twenty feet freely with the current, then, as the line tightens, he starts twitching the sunk fly with short pulls on the line until it hangs dead in the water below him. He feels that the free-drifting-and-sinking, first part of this presentation imitates a nymph that has lost its footing and is being swept downstream. The second, or dragging, part of this delivery, attempts to convince the trout that the fly, now rising and swinging up overhead, is a nymph swimming toward the surface to hatch out into an air-breathing, adult fly.

An even more sophisticated way to fish these flies is in an upstream manner, drag-free, the way you would fish a dry fly. This is probably the most advanced, difficult form of fly-fishing. It is also the most productive. An expert in this discipline can catch trout when all other fly-fishers are drawing blank.

An upstream nymph can fish quite deeply, especially if slightly weighted, because, the longer it drifts on a slack line, the farther down it sinks. A trout—even one with little desire to feed—will open its mouth and take a nymph that threatens to bang it on the nose. When water and weather conditions are utterly abominable, this is often the only method (short of live-bait fishing) to catch a few fish.

You can't cover much water fishing this way, so you'll also have to be an expert at reading currents. Concentrate on the known choicest lies where you can pin-point fish. Learning how quickly or slowly to recover line during each drift, to stay in touch with your fly, takes a lot of judgment and experience. So does detecting the slight pause in the downstream travel of your line, indicating that a fish might have taken your nymph. Such fishing demands the skill and concentration of a brain surgeon and very few anglers have the patience to master it.

WET-FLY AND NYMPH ON LAKES

This is the bread-and-butter method of catching trout in lakes and ponds and, fortunately, not a very demanding one. You cast your fly out over likely territory, or where you've caught fish before, and retrieve it with fairly slow twitches of several inches at a time. Outside of discovering where the trout are on that day, there are only two variations in this rather methodical technique that are left to your discretion.

One decision you have to make is at what depth your fly should travel. Some days (most likely, evenings) fish will take just under the surface where you can see the swirl of the strike. Other times, you may have to pause for several seconds and let your fly settle a few feet before starting your retrieve. When fishing is especially dour, you may have to resort to a leaded fly and a sinking line to fish near the bottom for a few, apathetic fish that weren't eager enough to swim up a few feet for a free meal. Generally speaking, if fish are feeding well, they'll take near the surface.

The speed of your retrieve is the other variable you'll have to consider. Sometimes tantalizingly slow is best, while on other occasions fish will prefer a fly that's stripped in quite briskly. You never know in advance. Experiment.

The only other lake fish with a fondness for sunk, insect-imitating flies are small bass and most panfish. The methods described, above, work well for them, too.

STREAMER-FLY ON RUNNING WATER

Trout not only love minnows, but, the bigger the fish, the higher the proportion of its smaller relatives that make up its diet. That's

A self-snagged (and useless) streamer fly.

why so many of those huge trout that stare down at you, glassy-eyed, from the wall were caught on bucktails or streamers. These flies imitate minnows and they're the trophy-fisher's (and the taxidermist's) best friend.

Streamers are usually fished in much the same way as wet flies, only with a bit more vigor. They are cast across and down-current at about a 45-degree angle to the flow and twitched or pumped in the current to act like a bait-minnow in distress. There's something about an injured or dying minnow that brings out the bully in both trout and bass.

There are two major points to keep in mind when fishing streamers. The first is that they're most effective in fast water—deep runs or heads of pools on modest flows. They're also strong medicine during the torrents of spring or when water levels are up after a summer rain. They're deadliest when they force the fish into making a snap decision.

The other thing to remember about streamers and bucktails is that a poorly timed cast can render them useless. The feathers or hair that make up their "wings" are typically twice as long as the hook-shank and, if these get snagged in the bend of the hook, fish won't touch the now off-kilter imitation. (You might think this would make the fly look and act even more like a crippled minnow, but somehow it doesn't.) On windy or gusty days, I always check my streamer after every few casts and it can't hurt to take a look every few minutes even on calm days. You can feel pretty stupid when you discover you've been casting for a half-hour with a fly that was completely out of commission.

STREAMERS ON STILLWATERS

Bucktails and streamers are probably the most productive flies for lake-dwelling trout, bass and pike. Two-inch flies are the usual choice for trout, three- to four-inchers for bass; and for pike, go for the biggest and brightest you can buy.

Again, fish them much as you would a wet fly on these waters, only a bit faster and with more pronounced twitches. Sometimes bass, which are inordinately fond of crawfish, will respond to a brownish fly, like the Muddler Minnow, fished slowly and just off the bottom on a sinking line. Pike, on the other hand, show a decided preference for a fast-moving fly.

SALT-WATER STREAMERS

Since most salt-water gamefish live on baitfish, streamers and bucktails are the mainstays of the sea-going fly-rodder. Big, pike-sized flies are almost always best, but they won't last long in the briny unless they're tied on stainless-steel hooks.

Most salt-water baitfish travel a lot faster than fresh-water ones so your retrieve should usually be brisk. This may mean that you'll have to cast out more often, but it will also mean more strikes.

In a few cases, you'll be hard pressed to move your fly rapidly enough. If fish keep following your fly, then turning away, try a more frenzied retrieve. Some barracuda specialists cast out, jam their rod handle between their legs and retrieve line hand-over-hand (yes, with both hands) like madmen. This takes some practice, but the barracuda eat it up.

71

FLY-FISHING THE FLATS

The flats are a world of their own. The fish that feed in this thin water and their food are different from most oceanic types. The bonefish, permit and redfish that cruise the shallows aren't looking for minnows, but for shrimps and crabs. This sort of food is not swift, but it manages to survive by concealment in the grass or by burrowing in the sand or mud when threatened.

Here, your fly should imitate not only the appearance of crabs or shrimps, but also their scuttling, secretive behavior. Such flies should be tied upside-down—that is, with most of the hair or feathers on the underside, instead of on top of, the hook-shank —so that the fly will ride hook-point up. A conventionally tied fly will hang up on the bottom or pick up weed too frequently to be useful here. It's best to cast your fly ten to fifteen feet ahead of a cruising fish, which will minimize your chances of alarming it in such shallow water. Give your fly a couple of good tugs to catch the fish's attention and to make it appear that it is trying to escape. Then, let your fly drop quickly to the bottom.

The fish, at this point, should swing over to investigate, but even if it doesn't, you have one last resort. Give your fly another sharp tug which should kick up sand or a puff of mud from the bottom. That should do it. Now, as the fish approaches, resist the temptation to overdo it and strip the fly again. The fish knows where the fly is, all right. Your job now is to make your imitation act as if it were trying to burrow out of sight.

Try to just jiggle the fly on the bottom. If the fish starts to turn away, twitch a little harder, but don't strip. Stay with your game plan. The fish may, indeed, refuse your fly. Flats fish—especially permit, but also heavily pounded bonefish—can be very picky. But scooting your fly rapidly along the bottom is, at this point, only going to look unrealistic and may, perhaps, alarm the fish. Most anglers manipulate their flats-flies far too much.

If the fish is a stationary tailer, your tactics should be slightly different. Cast as close to it as you dare or within, say, a foot or two, and in front of the fish. Let it sink and then twitch it ever

72

so slightly so that it acts like an animal that's been dislodged by the fish's rooting and is trying to dig down and hide again.

I can't promise you that you'll take every fish you cast to by following these instructions. You'll spook a lot no matter how careful you are. And some days the fish won't take anything. But you'll take your share of them, and a far higher percentage of fish you cast to, than the compulsive stripper will.

7
Hooking, Playing and Landing

". . . my bended hook shall pierce/Their slimy jaws . . ."

—William Shakespeare,
Antony and Cleopatra

Congratulations! You've done everything right so far and you've inveigled a fish into taking your fly. Now what?

SETTING THE HOOK

Artificial flies don't taste like natural food and most don't even have a similar texture so they're usually ejected by the fish shortly after they've been taken. However, some species of fish will mouth a fly longer, or take it in a different manner from others, so the art of hooking fish is one with several subtle variations.

Raise your rod quickly (but gently) to set the hook.

Running Water

Let's take the easiest case first. When you're fishing any type of sunk fly—nymph, wet fly or streamer—across and downstream in flowing water, your line is tight and you should strike the instant you feel a fish touch your fly. By this, I don't mean you should try to yank its head off. Over ninety percent of all trout broken off are lost through heavy-handed striking. A quick, but gentle, twitch of the wrist is enough to ensure that the hook is pulled in over the barb. In fact, the fish will often hook itself before you have time to react and nothing could be simpler than that.

However, when fishing wets and streamers in this standard manner, too many fish are missed. You feel a thump and they're gone before you have time to strike. This, unfortunately, is one of the drawbacks of this technique, but there is something you can do to hook a higher percentage of fish. Try to cast an absolutely straight line onto the water and to keep it straight, without bellying, during the swing. It's surprising how many more fish

76

you'll hook firmly when you're in direct contact with your fly at all times.

Striking a fish that takes a dry fly is quite different. Here, you should hook a much higher percentage of takers because, since you're casting upstream, you're pulling the fly back into the fish's mouth. (In downstream fishing, you're actually yanking the fly away from the fish.) And, since the fish isn't instantaneously pricked by the hook, you can afford a slight pause before striking.

Probably a fish that has risen up to the surface—a zone of jeopardy—wants to get back down to its lie before sorting out what it has managed to grab. Whatever the reason, trout will hold a dry fly in their mouths for as much as several seconds before spitting it out. British chalk-stream anglers maintain that, when a trout takes a floater, you should wait till after you've intoned, "God save the Queen" before striking.

I'll have to confess that at such moments I'm seldom preoccupied with the salvation of the Queen, but I do wait about a second before making contact. If you think of this act as more

Hand and line positions for wet-fly or streamer retrieve.

of a quick tightening than a true strike, you'll save a lot of flies and tippet material. The majority of anglers hit a rising fish both too quickly and too heftily.

You should be even more deliberate and tentative when fishing tiny dry flies (#18 or smaller) or the spent-wing imitations of dead mayflies at dusk. Both types of artificials are virtually impossible to see on the water so it's a mistake to rear back when you see a dimple or ring appear in the vicinity of your fly. If the trout has taken a nearby natural instead, ripping your fly across the water may put the fish down. If, on the other hand, the fish has taken, a hearty strike will all too often snap the leader. And if this happens in late evening, it's usually too dark to tie on another one. The best procedure here is to wait a second, raise your rod slowly and feel for contact with the fish. Slight rod-tension is usually enough to set these small hooks securely.

Still Waters
Wet and streamer fly-fishing on lakes calls for a different hook-setting technique. Twitch-retrieve with your left hand pulling the line. Don't try to add action by switching the rod tip. Your rod should stay motionless, pointing directly down the path of the line. After each draw, pinch the line under the forefinger of your right, or rod, hand (see illustration) so that it's always under tension. When you do feel a fish tighten, do *not* raise your rod tip for a conventional strike. Just keep retrieving at the same pace until the rod bucks and the fish takes off. Then raise your rod.

Why this is more effective than striking as you would in running water, I don't know. I have never been submerged with mask and snorkel nearby when a fish took a streamer in still water. But any Maine guide will promise you this is the surest way to hook trout, bass or landlocked salmon on wets and streamers and he's absolutely right.

Bass bugs and poppers, on the other hand, call for instant retaliation. The moment you see the swirl or splash of the fish, strike—and this time I really mean it. Most bugs are tied on big, heavy-wire hooks and it takes a healthy yank to pull this over the barb into a bass's tough mouth. A flabby strike will usually mean that your popper will be tossed free on the first, head-shaking jump.

While retrieving or manipulating your bug, point your rod straight down the line, exactly as you would when retrieving a streamer. Only this time, you should make the strike by both hauling back on the line with your left hand and raising your rod sharply. You can afford this strong, two-fisted strike because a bug leader is usually plenty strong.

It's almost impossible to strike too quickly and it's easy to strike too late. Only on those rare occasions when you see the fish swimming up under your bug could you snatch it away from him prematurely. Under usual sighting conditions, though, and with the relatively long line you're casting, the fish will have your bug firmly in its mouth and will already be headed for the bottom by the time your strike-energy reaches him.

Salt Water

Fishing streamers in salt water calls for much the same tactics you'd use on lakes, except everything is a bit more heroic and vigorous. You should be using a relatively strong leader in this game so there should be no worry about breakage. Once you feel the fish has fastened, rear back hard. Big, stainless-steel hooks don't penetrate easily, so hitting a fish hard and doing it even twice is good insurance.

Flats

Again, fish on the salt-water flats behave differently than other salt-water species. Usually, the only sign that a fish is taking your fly is a tilting of its head toward the bottom. You seldom feel the strike. But if the surface isn't too ruffled, you can see the fish nose down quite clearly. Wait a second or even two then draw in a foot or so of line slowly and feel for the fish. If he's still only looking, all is not lost as it would be with a full-fledged strike. With this tentative move, your fly will only scoot along the bottom for a foot or so and you're still in the ballgame.

79

If, however, you feel solid contact, strike hard and with both hands at the same time. Quickly do it again. In fact hit him three times if you can. Bonefish have leathery mouths. But hit them only during that short truce bonefish usually agree to before they realize they're in trouble. Once they start their dash, don't try to set the hook again. That would be risking a break-off—even with a stout 10- or 12-pound test tippet.

PLAYING A FISH

When it comes to playing and landing fish, the fly rod really shines. Being the most delicate and sensitive of rods, it magnifies the fight and transmits every throb and move of the fish intimately to the hand of the angler. A two-pound fish is more fun on the long rod than a four-pounder is on bait-casting or spinning tackle.

The fly rod is also the deadliest instrument. A long, supple rod cushions the shocks so that even a lightly hooked fish can usually be landed. And its greater leverage helps you guide the fish in the direction you want.

When stream or river fishing, try to conduct the fight from a position directly cross-current from the fish. This will tire him faster and tend to keep the hook firmly lodged. Keep your rod tip high and well bent at all times. If a sizable fish makes a determined run, relax pressure and let him go, pulling line off the reel. The minute the fish stops or turns, put the pressure back on again. Don't try to pull a fish back up-current, but follow rapidly till you're abreast of him again. Then, keep him working.

Always play a fish relatively hard. You'll be doing yourself and the fish a favor. By ''hard'' I don't mean ham-fisted horsing. But tire the fish out quickly (then either kill or release it) by applying steady pressure up near the limit of what your tippet and hook size can withstand. The longer you play a fish, the greater the chance of losing it and the poorer the odds of the fish recovering from the fight if released.

If a large fish tries to sulk in slack water, get him moving again

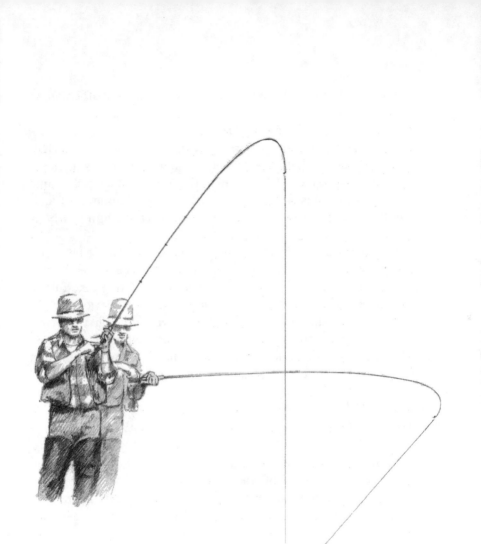

Hold rod-tip high when playing fish, but lower it to horizontal when fish is near you.

as soon as possible. Get below him and try to pull him off balance. Pluck the tight line to annoy him. Don't give him a breather or he'll get his second wind and prolong the fight.

Try to keep the fish working in a fairly strong current. Here he'll have to fight both the rod and the flow. When he's in close, hold your rod to the side, parallel to the water, but keep the same bend in it. It's this side pressure that makes swimming difficult and tiring. Pulling upward on a fish won't fatigue him nearly as much.

On ponds and lakes or in the ocean, currents can't help you tire a fish but your general tactics should be the same. Try to keep steady, even pressure at all times except during determined runs. Keep the fish on the move without any rest periods.

You can usually tell when a fish is playing out. First, its runs will get shorter and shorter until they're reduced to small surges. Then the fish will start rolling over on its side, an obvious sign of fatigue. Very soon now, you should be able to land it.

LANDING

Most fish are finally captured in a landing net, but if you forget to bring one or it's out of reach, you can beach fish—even quite large ones—if the terrain is suitable. Gaffing and tailing are now such rare, and often outlawed, methods that I won't describe them here.

Never try to land a fish by sweeping the net towards it. Make the fish swim into it, head first, while you hold it stationary. Submerge the rim just under the surface, tilted at a 30- to 45-degree angle, get the fish's head up on the surface and slowly lead or pull it over the net. Only when most or all of its body is over the bag should you lift the net.

In running water, it's best to face up-current, so the bag will extend downstream. This may mean that you'll have to step slightly down-current from the fish for this final maneuvre and bring him down to the net. Again, the fish's head should be on,

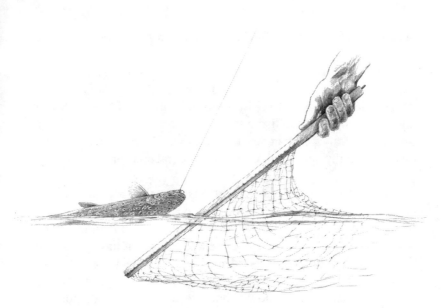

A tired trout being netted properly.

A captured—and pacified—bass.

or slightly above, the surface and fish seem more docile, or less likely to see the net, if they're also lying flat on their sides.

Bass, and perhaps a few larger panfish, can be landed by an easy method involving no extra equipment. As a played-out fish comes within reach, put your thumb in its mouth, bend the lower jaw down, and pull the fish out of the water. This lower-jaw grip seems to paralyze, or at least tranquilize, bass. Never attempt this with toothy species like pike and barracuda for obvious reasons.

Beaching is a tricky, last-resort business that is only possible on accommodating terrain. You'll need a gently sloping beach or cobble shallows and at least twenty feet of room behind you. When the fish is on its side in the shallows, point the rod toward the fish with only a slight bend in it and start backing up.

If the fish panics and heads for deeper water, as it often will, let it go. Then bring it slowly back to the original position, its head directly toward you and start backing steadily up the beach. Once the fish's body hits the sand or gravel, it will usually start

flopping. Now, if you keep applying firm, steady pressure by backing up more rapidly, the fish will keep "swimming" on dry land till it's a safe distance above water line. Admittedly, this game takes a little practice, but it comes in handy and sometimes it's the only game in town.

8

How to Become Expert

"Practice . . . practice . . . practice!"

—Paul Hornung

As I stated in an early chapter, I don't believe a beginner can learn fly-casting or fly-fishing from a standing start by reading any book. There are just too many subtle points that can only be learned from demonstration and observation. Yet I am equally convinced that reading is one of the surest ways to improve your performance once you've mastered the basics. Again, let me recommend the books listed in Appendix 5. Video cassettes can help, too, but they don't offer anything like the wealth of information you'll find in a good angling library.

There are several excellent outdoor magazines that can keep you posted on new fly patterns and innovative presentations. Some of these flies and techniques may not prove helpful on the waters you fish, but somebody has worked hard to develop them and believes they're superior, so they're worth a try.

You may also profit from joining a local chapter of Trout

Unlimited, Federation of Fly Fishers or some other angling club. (See Appendix 5) You can learn a lot from listening to fellow members—not the least of which may be new and better places to fish.

By all means practice casting as often as you can, at least until you're an intermediate fly-fisher or better. Only when you can cast proficiently and automatically can you concentrate fully on the fish and on your presentation.

Field study can pay big dividends, too. Learn all you can about water and currents. Study depth charts of nearby lakes and coastlines. Collect and examine the insects, minnows and crustaceans your fish feed on and observe their behavior.

By all means, keep a fishing diary. After each trip, jot down weather and water conditions, area fished, fish seen, fish caught, flies used, failures and successes. What natural insects did you see? How did they behave? How did fish rise to them? Re-read your notes from time to time. It's surprising how much you can learn from your own experiences.

It is extremely important to acquire the best flies possible. Not the most, just the very best. I know anglers who have spent many thousands of dollars for big collections of expensive rods and reels, yet their fly boxes are filled with junk. I can't comprehend this. Fish can't be impressed by rods and reels. The only part of your tackle they're ever supposed to see, after all, is the fly at the very end of it all.

I wish I could tell you how to judge a superb fly from a poor one, but there are just too many types of flies. Words might not be too helpful, anyway, because some qualities defy description. Therefore, my best advice is to find out who ties, or carries, the best flies in your area and then get an expert friend to help you make a selection.

There are no written rules on behavior or etiquette for fly-fishers but there is a general consensus on some Do's and Don't's. Most of these spring from a simple respect for the environment or for your fellow angler and are so close to good manners in general that I almost hesitate to mention them.

Don't leave litter and don't trespass on private property unless you've first asked for permission. Every year, more and more private land is posted against public access and the above two offenses are usually given as the reasons.

Since fish are a finite resource—yes, even in salt water—kill only fish you want to eat. Snook and striped bass populations have recently become alarmingly low. Tarpon, sailfish and bonefish are poor eating and should not be killed just to satisfy a "show-and-tell" vanity. Release all undersized or unwanted fish with tender loving care so that they may live to be caught again.

Keep a respectful distance between yourself and other anglers. This is as true for boat fishermen as it is for those afoot. There are, unfortunately, no laws or penalties against roaring up to a school of surface-feeding fish, cutting the throttle at the last instant and driving the fish down and away from other fishermen who were there first, but it's obviously slob behavior.

Similarly, when fishing a stream, especially smallish ones, give the angler there ahead of you the courtesy of his obvious priority. Don't crowd in close to him. If he's fishing downstream, start a decent distance upstream of him. Grant him the same deference and space if he's fishing upstream by starting in well downstream.

Lastly, you don't have to be an expert to get great enjoyment out of fly-fishing. But I think you'll agree that, the better your performance in any sport, the more pleasure you get from it. So, I would now like to think that, since you've read this far, you're already a bit more proficient at fly-fishing and that you will find it even more rewarding.

APPENDIX 1

Hook Size Chart

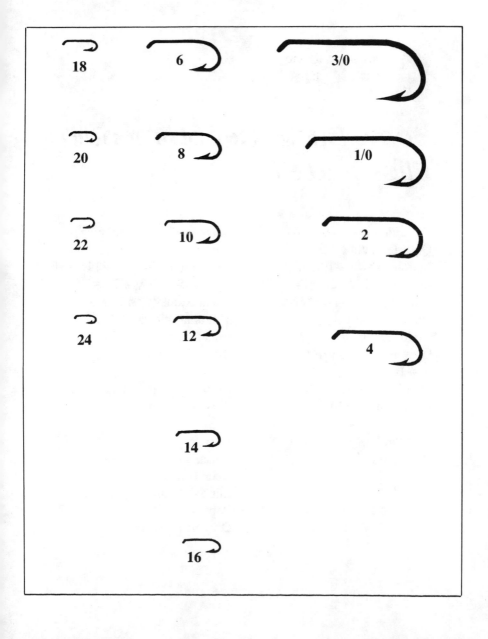

APPENDIX 2

Some Basic, Recommended Flies and Sizes

Dry Flies
Quill Gordon #12, #14
March Brown #10, #12
Light Cahill #12, #14, #16
Adams #12, #14, #16
Hair-wing Royal
  Coachman #12, #14, #16
Grey Fox Variant #12, #14,
  #16
Dun Variant #12, #14
Blue Caddis #14, #16
Tan Caddis #14, #16, #18
Henryville #14, #16, #18
Black Ant #12, #14

Nymphs
Cream #12, #14, #16
Tan #12, #14, #16

Black #12, #14, #16
Hare's Ear #10, #12, #14
Pheasant Tail #12, #14, #16
Yellow Stonefly #8, #10
Black Stonefly, #6, #8
Montana #8, #10
Breadcrust #12, #14
Blue Caddis Emerger #12,
  #14
Brown Caddis Emerger #12,
  #14

Bass Bugs
(Small, Medium and Large)
Deer Hair Frog
Injured Minnow
Popper
Dragon Fly Bug

Wet Flies
Gold-ribbed Hare's Ear #12, #14
Leadwing Coachman, #10, #12
Royal Coachman #10, #12, #14
March Brown #10, #12
Light Cahill #12, #14, #16
Black Gnat #12, #14
Blue Dun #12, #14, #16

Streamers
(Sizes #2–#10, long-shank)
Muddler Minnow
Mickey Finn
Grey Ghost
Black-nosed Dace
Nine-three

Black Marabou
Yellow Marabou
White Marabou
Black Ghost

Salt Water
White Deceiver #2/0, #2
Blue/White Deceiver #2/0, #2
Yellow Deceiver #2/0, #2
Tarpon Special #3/0
White Skipping Bug #2/0

Flats
Pink Shrimp #2, #4, #6
Honey Blonde #2, #4, #6
Crazy Ike (White) #2, #4, #6
Crazy Ike (Tan) #2, #4, #6

APPENDIX 3

Recommended Leader Tippet Strength By Fly Size

Fly-hook Size	Diameter (in thousandths of an inch)	Pound Test
20, 22, 24	.004	2
16, 18, 20	.005	3
12, 14, 16	.006	4
10, 12, 14	.007	5
8, 10, 12	.008	6
4, 6, 8	.009	7
1/0, 2, 4	.010	8.5
1/0 to 5/0	.011+	10 to 15

APPENDIX 4

Fly-Fisherman's Check List

Necessities	*Useful Extras*	*Optional*
Rod	Stream thermometer	Wader repair kit
Reel (with line)	Vest	Rod repair kit
Leader	Rain jacket	Aquarium net
Fly boxes	Spare reel (with line)	Specimen bottles
Tippet material	Extra leaders	Knot-tying tool
Floatant	Line dressing	Long-nosed
Boots (or waders)	Leader straightener	pliers
Hat	Leader sink	First aid kit
Polaroids (or glasses)	Hook hone	Camera
Nail clipper or scissors	Hemostat	Flask (full)
License	Wading staff	
First Cast	Stiletto (for	
	picking out knots)	

APPENDIX 5

Recommended Reading

BOOKS
Art Flick's Master Fly-Tying Guide by Art Flick et al. Crown, 1972, Nick Lyons Books, 1984. Experts share their fly-tying tricks and techniques.
Caddisflies by Gary LaFontaine. Nick Lyons Books, 1979. Possibly more than you want to know about these aquatic insects—but it's nice to know it's all there.
Fly-Fishing in Salt Water by Lefty Kreh. Nick Lyons Books, 1974. Tackle and tactics for the big ones in the briny.
Hatches by Al Caucci and Bob Nastasi. Comparahatch, Ltd., 1975. Word and color-photo guide to North American mayflies.
Lamar Underwood's Bass Almanac. Nick Lyons Books, 1979. Experts reveal their secrets for taking America's most popular gamefish.
Masters on the Dry Fly ed. by J. Migel. Lippincott, 1977. Top dry-fly men give a detailed ''how-to'' course.
Masters on the Nymph ed. by J. Migel and L. Wright. Nick

Lyons Books, 1979. Mysteries of successful nymph-fishing explained by master nymphers.

A Modern Dry-Fly Code by Vincent Marinaro. Nick Lyons Books, 1983. Flies and tactics for fishing limestoners and spring creeks.

The Orvis Fly-fishing Guide by Tom Rosenbauer. Nick Lyons Books, 1984. Complete and clear—ideal for the beginning or intermediate fly-fisher.

Selective Trout by Doug Swisher and Carl Richards. Crown, 1971, Nick Lyons Books, 1985. How to outwit smart and choosy trout.

Stillwater Trout ed. by J. Merwin. Nick Lyons Books, 1980. Special techniques and winning flies for ponds and lakes.

Trout by Ray Bergman. Knopf, 1938. After nearly fifty years, still some of the best and wisest advice.

MAGAZINES

The Flyfisher, 1387 Cambridge, Idaho Falls, ID 83401. Official magazine of the Federation of Fly Fishers.

Flyfishing, P.O. Box 02112, Portland, OR 97202. Fly-fishing and fly-tying with emphasis on the West.

Fly Fisherman, 2245 Kohn Road, Box 8200, Harrisburg PA 17105. Timely articles by top anglers on flies, tackle, tactics and places.

Rod and Reel, Box 679, Camden ME 04843. Feature articles on the world of fly-fishing.

Trout, P.O. Box 6225, Bend OR 97708. The official journal of Trout Unlimited.

RECOMMENDED JOINING

Federation of Fly Fishers, P.O. Box 1088, West Yellowstone MT 59758. Over 200 chapters so there must be one near you.

Trout Unlimited, 501 Church Street, NE, Vienna, VA 22180. Emphasis on trout and trout habitat conservation in the U.S. and Canada.

APPENDIX 6

Gamefish Temperature and Food Preferences

Fish	Temperature	Food
	Fresh Water	
Trout	Cool, 50s, 60s	Insects, minnows
Bass (Smallmouth)	Medium, 60s, 70s	Crawfish, minnows, insects
Bass (Largemouth)	Warm, 70s, 80s	Small fish, crawfish, frogs
Pike	Medium, 60s, 70s	Small fish
Pickerel	Medium 60s, 70s	Small fish
Bluegill	Warm, 70s, 80s	Insects
Yellow Perch	Warm, 70s, 80s	Insects, minnows
	Salt Water	
Striped Bass	Medium, 60s, 70s	Small fish
Bluefish	Medium, 60s, 70s	Small fish
Mackerel	Medium, 60s, 70s	Small fish
Barracuda	Warm, 70s, 80s	Fish
Snook	Warm, 70s, 80s	Small fish, shrimp
Tarpon	Warm, 70s, 80s	Small fish

	Flats	
Bonefish	Warm, 70s, 80s	Shrimp, crabs
Permit	Warm, 70s, 80s	Crabs, shrimp
Redfish	Warm, 70s, 80s	Shrimp, crabs, minnows

APPENDIX 7

A Glossary of Common Fly-Fishing Terms

Aquatic insects. Insects such as mayflies, caddisflies and stone-flies that spend their early lives underwater.

Back-cast. That portion of the common, overhead cast when the line is propelled to the rear, behind the angler.

Backing-line. Strong, thin, usually braided line put on the reel before the fly line to fill out the spool and for insurance in case a fish makes a long run.

Belly. The fattest, heaviest portion of a tapered fly line. Also, any pronounced curve in the position of the extended fly line.

Current-tongue. The thread, or fastest part, of any current.

Drag. Any influence on fly line or leader that makes a fly travel at a speed different from the current or flow.

Drift-food. Any food item, usually an insect or crustacean, that is floating on, or suspended in, the water.

Drown. A dry fly or a floating line is said to ''drown'' when it gets pulled under the water surface.

Dry Fly. A fly, usually quite bushy in appearance, that is tied to exploit surface tension and float on top of the water.

Eddy. Any small or large whirlpool on flowing water.

False cast. Any cast where the line is kept in the air and not allowed to fall on the water.

Fast-action rod. A fly rod that flexes mostly near the tip so that, when bent, it snaps back to a straight position relatively quickly.

Floating line. A fly line with a density lighter than water so that it will float without greasing.

Fly floatant. A water-repellant paste or liquid that helps a dry fly float higher and longer.

Forward cast. The second part of a regular cast where the line is propelled forward and in front of the angler.

Hatch. As a verb, an aquatic insect's shedding of its nymphal shuck (usually on the water surface) and becoming a winged adult. As a noun, that period of time (often too brief) when many insects are on the water.

Leader. A length of less-visible monofilament (usually tapered) between the heavier fly line and the fly.

Lie. The fairly stationary feeding or holding position of a fish in running water.

Limestone stream. A usually slow-moving, often weedy stream that has a high pH and is rich in fish food.

Line speed. The speed at which the unstraightened part of a fly line (and the fly) is travelling during a cast.

Monofilament. A single-strand, transparent material, usually of nylon, that is used for leaders.

Natural. The real insect or crustacean that fish feed on as opposed to the angler's imitation.

Open loop. A wide curve in the fly line as it travels forward or backward during casting.

Overhead cast. The most common cast in fly-fishing, in which the rod is held in a vertical, or near-vertical, position.

Pocket. A miniature pool in a run or riffle, usually created by an emerging rock or boulder.

Pool. A slow, deep portion of a river or stream where the gradient temporarily levels out.

Presentation. The manner in which a fly lands on the water and how it is made to behave in the fishing area.

Prick. To scratch, or hook only momentarily, a fish that has taken the fly. Such fish will rarely strike a second time.

Power stroke. That brief period during a forward or backward cast when power is applied by the rod hand.

Read. The act of analyzing a stream or river from clues provided by depth, cover and currents to determine where the fish should lie.

Riffle. A fast portion of running water, usually shallow and containing few good fish.

Rise. The upward motion of a fish toward either a natural or artificial food item—usually, but not always, breaking the surface.

Rise-form. The disturbance left on the surface by a rising fish. This is most often a spreading circle.

Roll cast. A maneuvre in which the line is rolled out over the water without any back-cast.

Rough stream. Also spate, rainfed or freestone stream. These are usually characterized by rubble and boulder streambeds, rather steep gradients and frequent flooding. The majority of our streams fall into this category.

Rubble. Stones larger than gravel, but smaller than slabs or boulders.

Run. A fast portion of stream or river, narrower and deeper than a riffle. These are good trout-holding places, especially in summer.

Running line. The thin portion of any weight-forward fly line behind the belly.

Shoot. To let out extra line during the forward or backward cast to increase the distance of a cast.

Sidearm cast. Precisely the same as the overhead cast except that all motions are carried out in a more horizontal plane.

Sinking line. All fly lines with a specific gravity heavier than water. There are now an astonishing variety—from ultra-fast sinkers to slow, medium and fast sinkers—including various ones where the body of the line floats and only the end portion sinks.

Slow-action rod. A fly rod that bends down into the grip when flexed. Such rods are slower in their snap-back time and aren't so demanding of perfect timing on the part of the caster.

Spring creek. A usually slow-moving stream from sand country—not as rich as a limestoner, but having many of the same qualities.

Stillwater. A pond or lake. Any body of water where current is not a factor.

Strike. The act of a fish taking a fly. Also the angler's reaction to set the hook when a fish has taken.

Strip. To pull in line, after the cast has been made with the left, or line, hand to manipulate the fly in a series of jerks.

Sunk fly. Any fly fished below the surface: wet flies, nymphs, streamers, bucktails.

Tailing. When fish are bottom-feeding in shallow water, their tails often break the surface. Such easily spotted fish are called "tailers."

Tailing loop. When the loop formed by the unrolling fly line has an arc greater than 180 degrees, it has a "closed" or "tailing" loop. This is the greatest cause of casting knots into a leader.

Tight loop. If the loop formed by the unrolling fly line is two feet wide or less, it can be considered "tight." If it measures three feet or more, it is "open."

Tippet. The last and thinnest strand of a tapered leader—the one to which the fly is tied.

Traveling loop. The loop formed by an unrolling fly line.